NOV 0 6 2017

P9-BIK-617

# weekend QUILTING

### Quilt and Unwind with Simple Designs to Sew in No Time

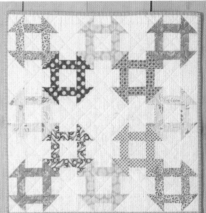

Jemima Flendt

Fons&Porter

NAPA COUNTY LIBRARY
580 COOMBS STREET
NAPA, CA 94559

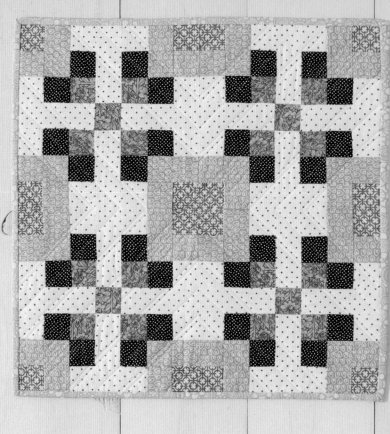

Weekend Quilting. Copyright © 2017 by Jemima Flendt. Manufactured in China. All rights reserved. The patterns and drawings in this book are for the personal use of the reader. By permission of the author and publisher, they may be either hand-traced or photocopied to make single copies, but under no circumstances may they be resold or republished. No other part of this book may be reproduced in any form or by any electronic or mechanical means including information storage and retrieval systems without permission in writing from the publisher, except by a reviewer who may quote brief passages in a review. Published by Fons & Porter Books, an imprint of F+W Media, Inc., 10151 Carver Road, Suite 200, Blue Ash, Ohio 45242. (800) 289-0963. First Edition.

**fw**

a content + ecommerce company

www.fwcommunity.com

21 20 19 18 17   5 4 3 2 1

Distributed in Canada by Fraser Direct
100 Armstrong Avenue
Georgetown, ON, Canada L7G 5S4
Tel: (905) 877-4411

Distributed in the U.K. and Europe by
F&W MEDIA INTERNATIONAL
Pynes Hill Court, Pynes Hill, Rydon Lane
Exeter, EX2 5AZ, United Kingdom
Tel: (+44) 1392 797680
E-mail: enquiries@fwmedia.com

**SRN:** R0175
**ISBN-13:** 978-1-4402-4661-6

**EDITOR:** Jodi Butler

**TECHNICAL  EDITOR:** Debra Fehr Greenway

**ART DIRECTOR:** Nicola DosSantos

**DESIGNER:** Amanda Murray

**ILLUSTRATOR:** Angela Pullen Atherton

**PHOTOGRAPHERS:** George Boe and Jemima Flendt

# Contents

# Introduction

Sewing and crafting have been an important part of my life since I was a young girl. I developed a love of sewing early from my nanna, who encouraged me to sew with her leftover scraps. She and I would spend hours crafting together while she taught me how to sew and crochet. I remember when I was sixteen bundling up my mom's leftover fabric and feeling inspired to make a quilt. Mom took me to quilting lessons, and I haven't stopped since. My love for quilting and sewing has continued to grow throughout my life. It has become not only my hobby but also my full-time passion.

I love teaching others to quilt and sew. I enjoy watching people begin their journey as well as make progress and amazing projects along the way. Showing, sharing, and passing along knowledge is at the core of what quilting is about. Before I started quilting and designing full-time, I was a high school home economics teacher. I never dreamed that I would leave teaching to pursue a career as a quiltmaker and designer. These days, I create quilts and sewing projects for publications worldwide as well as patterns for my own label, Tied with a Ribbon. I teach quilting in my hometown and travel nationally and internationally to teach quilting and sewing at weekend retreats and seminars.

My own two girls are now very much involved with my quilting and designing. Whether I'm taking inspiration from their drawings or letting them help pull fabrics for a project, I love having them in my sewing studio, making, creating, and designing themselves.

In my home there are quilts everywhere—on beds and couches, displayed on ladders, and even hung on walls. Quilts have become my life, and I wouldn't have it any other way.

Knowing that time spent sewing is a luxury these days, I believe that the time you do spend sewing should not only be enjoyable but productive. With that in mind, the quilts and projects in this book were designed for you to create over a weekend. Many of the projects can be made for your home or as a gift. With everyone leading such busy lives these days, taking the time to make something by hand should be treasured because each "perfectly imperfect" stitch has been made with purpose and care.

The techniques I've included in this book are an introduction to just some of the ways in which you can make blocks. Once you've learned the basic techniques, you can create stunning projects and build on your skills as you go. These projects are suitable for beginners as well as experienced quilters looking for inspiration. They will help grow your quilting and sewing knowledge one project at a time with lots of tips and techniques along the way.

Enjoy!

Jemima

# CHAPTER 1

# Quiltmaking Basics

It's easy to learn the basics of quiltmaking and sewing. You just need a handful of fabrics and some equipment. By starting with smaller projects, you can quickly master skills and progress to larger, more complicated ones as your skills grow.

I teach a lot of beginning quilters and sewers, and one thing I usually get asked is where to start when purchasing a machine and equipment. Often people are worried about spending money on a new hobby they aren't sure they will like or enjoy. Although you don't have to spend a lot on a machine or equipment, I always suggest you buy the best your budget will allow. Cheap machines and equipment can be more work to use, and the results may not be what you planned.

If you are frustrated by your machine and equipment, it can be hard to enjoy what you are doing. A good-quality machine and tools will go a long way to helping you enjoy the experience and wanting to continue.

I don't have a lot of gadgets. I prefer to use tried and tested tools that do the job well. On the following pages, you'll find a list of my favorite tools as well as tips for making the time you spend quilting and sewing more enjoyable.

When you have time, visit your local quilt store to see the fabrics and equipment. Be sure to talk to the staff. They can help answer any additional questions you have and even help with fabric selection.

## TOOLS AND EQUIPMENT

Having the right tools will help ensure your quilting success and ultimately make your sewing experience more enjoyable. Here's my must-have list.

- Sewing machine with 1/4" (6 mm) foot. Having machine feet, such as a zipper foot (for installing zippers) and an open toe foot (for foundation paper piecing and appliqué), will also come in handy.

- Machine sewing needles

- Handsewing needles for handquilting and appliqué

- Rotary cutter and extra blades

- Self-healing cutting mat

- Clear acrylic rulers: 6½" × 24" (16.5 cm × 61 cm), 4½" (11.5 cm) square, and 6½" (16.5 cm) square

- Half-Square Triangle ruler (I like the Bloc Loc Half Square Triangle Square Up Ruler)

- Equilateral triangle ruler

- Seam ripper

- Scissors

- Binding clips

- Paper for foundation paper piecing (standard copy paper is fine)

- Paper-backed fusible web for appliqué projects

- Erasable fabric marking pens

- Fabric pencil

- Masking tape (low tack): 1/4" (6 mm) wide is great for handquilting and 1" (2.5 cm) works for basting quilts

- Curved safety pins

- Iron and ironing board

## CHOOSING FABRIC

**Note:** *All of the yardage in this book is based on 42" (106.5 cm) wide fabric.*

Choosing fabrics can be the most daunting part of the quilting process. These days, fabric designers create curated collections with coordinating colors and prints so you can easily create projects from a single range of fabric. However, sometimes you may want to start with a main fabric as a focal print, then coordinate the other fabrics around it. Be sure to match each additional color and print with the main fabric. Think about the person you're making the project for and choose fabrics you know they will love. Your confidence will grow as you choose more and more fabrics for projects.

I usually work with a variety of fabrics, including 100 percent cotton, linen, lawn, denim, chambray, and flannel. Often there may be several different types of fabric within one project. If you are starting out, stick to 100 percent quilters cotton. As your skills grow, you can incorporate other fabrics into projects to add texture and interest.

After you've made a few projects, your scrap basket will likely grow (mine is overflowing). I love scraps, and many of the projects in this book can incorporate pieces from your scrap basket. It feels great to use them up, and scraps can also give projects a unique look because you can create unexpected color palettes and designs.

## WASHING FABRIC

Washing fabric causes much debate among quilters. I don't prewash fabric before I start quilting, unless it is a color that may bleed, such as black, red, or navy. If you don't prewash your fabric, adding a color catcher sheet when washing your quilt can help take care of any excess dye in the water.

## THREAD

Use good-quality, 100 percent cotton thread whenever possible. It's frustrating to spend all of that time making a project only to have the thread let you down by breaking, snapping, or shredding. I prefer to use Aurifil 50wt thread for piecing and machine quilting. For handquilting, I like to use an Aurifil 12wt thread. The colors are amazing, and I can coordinate them for every project.

## SEWING MACHINE NEEDLES

For general quilting and sewing projects, use a universal size 80 needle. Change your needle for each new quilt top or after every 8 hours of sewing time. Having a nice sharp needle will ensure the tip moves smoothly through fabric, which can help prevent snagging, skipping, and pulling.

For sewing fabrics such as lawn, you will need a finer size 70 needle. If you are sewing with heavier fabrics, such as denim, you will need to change your needle to a size 90. Changing the needle to suit the fabric you are working with ensures that your sewing machine can easily sew through the fabrics—and helps avoid frustration.

## CUTTING

I like to cut fabrics using a rotary cutter and a self-healing cutting mat. These mats are far gentler on blades and will help keep them sharper longer. To ensure ease of cutting, change your rotary cutter blades often.

Using large 24" (61 cm) rulers will make it easier to cut the longest lengths from your fabric. I used Bloc Loc rulers for many of the projects in this book. I think they are worth the investment and will help you achieve far more accurate cutting when trimming blocks to size.

## SEAM ALLOWANCES

Always sew with a ¼" (6 mm) seam allowance. The best way to achieve this is by using a ¼" (6 mm) foot on your sewing machine. Match raw edges together and line up the edge of the fabric with the edge of the machine foot. When all of the seams are the same, correct size, the fabric pieces should fit together easily, and seams should match up neatly.

## PRESSING

We often refer to "pressing" in quilting rather than "ironing." Pressing means you lift and lower the iron onto the area that needs to be pressed, rather than pushing it across the fabric as you do with ironing. Pressing will help ensure that you do not distort the fabric weave or shape of the fabric. Pressing fabric correctly makes for a better-finished quilt top. For best results, press fabric before you start sewing. This helps ensure that if shrinkage occurs, it will happen before you cut out your pieces rather than after you have cut them to size. Also, always try to press fabric on the wrong side.

When setting seams, press the sewn seam first (**Figure 1**), before pressing the seam in the correct direction (**Figure 2**). This allows the stitches to meld together and holds the fabric better. It also helps alleviate distortion or stretching when you press your seams in one direction or another.

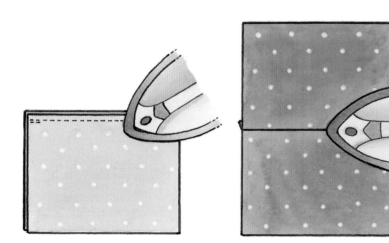
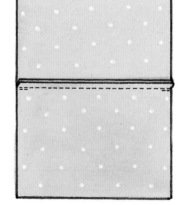

FIGURE 1    FIGURE 2 (front)    FIGURE 2 (back)

Generally, when you press seams to one side, press them toward the darker fabric. If you are using fabrics that have a white or light background against dark fabrics, it is often best to press seams open so you don't have dark shadows behind lighter fabrics in your project.

## TIPS FOR SUCCESS

Save time and effort with these simple strategies.

- Read the instructions thoroughly before you begin.

- Prewind your bobbins, so you can quickly reload in the middle of a project.

- Always pin before you begin sewing. It will help you avoid ripping out seams later.

- Have spare sewing machine needles handy.

- Make sure you have all of the sewing notions you will need to finish a project, such as zippers.

- Backstitch at the beginning and end of seams for durability.

- Keep a small pair of scissors near your sewing machine for snipping threads.

- Use precut fabric, if possible. This can help you save time and money.

- Keep your sewing machine manual handy. You never know when you will need it.

- Use leftover batting scraps from larger quilt projects. They are often a good size for pillows and can save you from having to run out and buy more batting for the projects in this book.

# CHAPTER 2

# The Nine Patch

Nine Patch blocks are simple, versatile blocks that add striking visuals to quilts and projects. You can limit the color range to only two fabrics or use up to nine prints or solids to make each design different.

The projects in this chapter are easy to sew. By following the pinning and pressing tips, you will have beautiful straight sewn lines, which are essential for Nine Patch blocks.

Although I have shown you only a couple of ways to design your blocks, you can add your own style by mixing up the arrangement of the squares to create new patterns. Both the Hopscotch Mini Quilt and Opposites Attract Pillow use variations on a Nine Patch block, and you can achieve very different looks by playing with the arrangements.

# How to Make a Two-Color Nine Patch Block

To make a Nine Patch block using two colors, you will need 6 strips of fabric that are the exact same size, 3 in one fabric (fabric A) and 3 in another (fabric B).

*All seam allowances are 1/4" (6 mm) unless otherwise noted.*

**1** Cut the strips to the required size for your project. Arrange as shown (**Figure 1**).

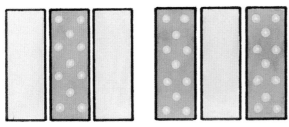

FIGURE 1

**2** Sew each set of 3 strips together to make 2 strip sets (**Figure 2**). Press the seams toward the darker fabric.

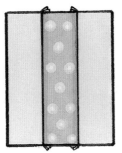
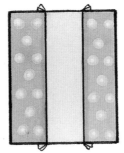

FIGURE 2

**3** Subcut each strip set into 3 units at the required width. Arrange 1 unit from the first strip set and 2 units from the second strip as shown (**Figure 3**).

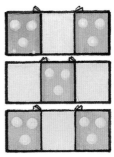

FIGURE 3

**4** Pin and sew the rows together (**Figure 4**). **Note:** *The pressed seams should nest neatly in the completed Nine Patch block.*

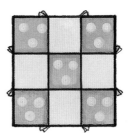

FIGURE 4

**5** Repeat steps 3 and 4 with the remaining strip set units to create a second Nine Patch block.

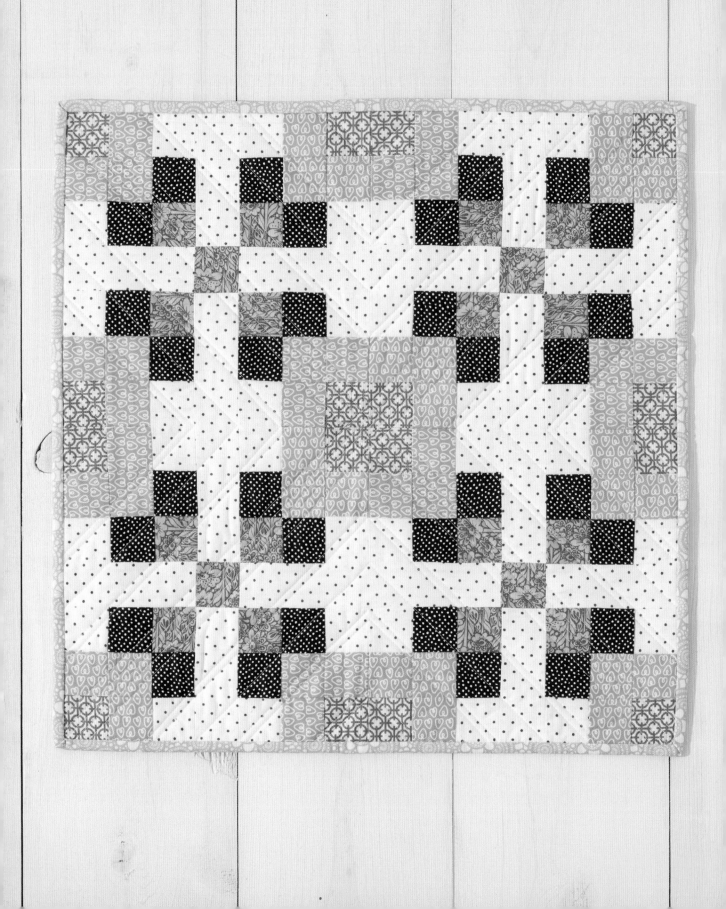

# Hopscotch Mini Quilt

It's easy to change the look of Nine Patch blocks by mixing up the fabric placement and limiting the colors to create a bold design. The Nine Patch blocks in this project are rotated to create the pattern. Paired with saturated colors, this quilt really stands out from the crowd.

## MATERIALS

Pink prints, 2 fat eighths (each 9" × 21" [23 cm × 53.5 cm]) (fabrics A, D)

Dark blue print, 1 fat eighth (9" × 21" [23 cm × 53.5 cm]) (fabric B)

Aqua print, 1/4 yard (0.2 m) (fabric C)

White/blue dot print, 3/8 yard (0.3 m) (fabric E)

Backing fabric, 30" (76 cm) square

Binding fabric, 1/4 yard (0.2 m)

Batting, 30" (76 cm) square

**Finished Size:**
21½" (54.5 cm) square

**Finished Block Size:**
4½" (11.5 cm) square

**FAT-EIGHTH FRIENDLY**

*All seam allowances are ¼" (6 mm) unless otherwise noted.*

## CUTTING INSTRUCTIONS

**From the first pink print (fabric A), cut:**

(2) 2" (5 cm) × WOF (width-of-fabric) strips

(4) 2" (5 cm) squares

**From the dark blue print (fabric B), cut:**

(4) 2" (5 cm) × WOF strips

**From the aqua print (fabric C), cut:**

(6) 2" × 21" (5 cm × 53.5 cm) strips

**From the second pink print (fabric D), cut:**

(2) 2" (5 cm) × WOF strips

**From the white/blue dot print (fabric E), cut:**

(4) 2" × 21" (5 cm × 53.5 cm) strips

(1) 2" (5 cm) × WOF strip; subcut into (4) 2" × 9½" (5 cm × 24 cm) rectangles

(1) 2" (5 cm) × WOF strip; subcut into (8) 2" × 5" (5 cm × 12.5 cm) rectangles

**From the binding fabric, cut:**

(3) 2½" (6.5 cm) × WOF strips

## MAKING THE BLOCKS

For detailed directions, see How to Make a Two-Color Nine Patch Block at the beginning of Chapter Two.

**1** Arrange the 2" (5 cm) print strips in this order:

Set 1: 1 A strip, 1 B strip, and 1 E strip

Set 2: 1 B strip and 2 C strips

Set 3: 1 E strip, 1 C strip, and 1 D strip

Sew the strips together along the long edges (**Figure 1**). Repeat to make a second set of strips for each set. Cut each strip set into (16) 2" (5 cm) wide units.

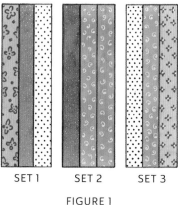

SET 1     SET 2     SET 3

FIGURE 1

**2** Sew 3 units together as shown to make a Nine Patch block (**Figure 2**). The current block size is 5" (12.5 cm) square. Make 16 blocks.

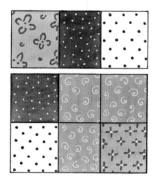
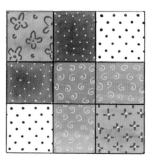

FIGURE 2

## ASSEMBLING THE QUILT

**3** Arrange the 16 Nine Patch blocks, the white/blue dot rectangles (all lengths), and 2" (5 cm) pink squares as shown (**Figure 3**).

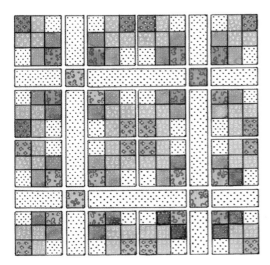

FIGURE 3

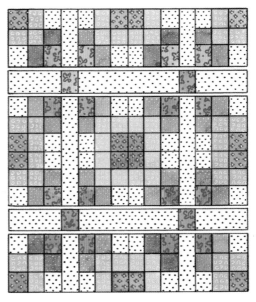

FIGURE 4

**4** Referring to **Figure 4** and working from left to right, pin and sew the first row together, then press the seams open. Pin and sew the second row of white/blue dot print rectangles and pink squares together, pressing the seams open. For the third row, pin and sew the first pair of Nine Patch blocks together vertically as shown, pressing the seams open, before sewing on the next white/blue dot print rectangle and continuing down the row.

**5** Sew the fourth and fifth row as you did in step 4.

**6** Pin and sew the completed rows together. Press the seams open.

**7** Layer the backing (wrong-side up), the batting, and the quilt top (right-side up), and baste them together. Quilt as desired. (The featured quilt was machine-quilted by sewing diagonal lines across the center, then sewing pointed lines into each of the sides.)

**8** Bind the quilt.

*For tips and detailed instructions on finishing your quilt, turn to Chapter Ten: Putting It All Together.*

# Opposites Attract Pillow

Nine Patch designs can be sewn up quickly and are an easy way to make over a pillow with just a few fabrics—or as many as you'd like! This Opposites Attract Pillow includes nine different prints. Make multiple pillows for any space needing some color.

## MATERIALS (FOR EACH PILLOW)

Assorted prints, 9 fat eighths
(each 9" × 21" [23 cm × 53.5 cm])

Background fabric, 1 fat quarter
(18" × 21" [45.5 cm x 53.5 cm])

Pillow backing fabric, 2/3 yard (0.6 m)

Binding fabric, 1/4 yard (0.2 m)

Batting, 26" (66 cm) square

Zipper, 18" (45.5 cm)

Pillow insert, 18" (45.5 cm) square

**Note:** *To make both pillows, you will need to double the Materials list requirements, then follow the Make a Four-Block Opposites Attract Pillow instructions.*

**Finished Size:**
18½" (47 cm) square

**Finished Block Size:**
6" (15 cm) square

**FAT-EIGHTH FRIENDLY**

*All seam allowances are ¼" (6 mm) unless otherwise noted.*

## CUTTING INSTRUCTIONS

**From each of the 9 assorted prints, cut:**
(1) 2½" (6.5 cm) × WOF (width-of-fabric) strip

**From the background fabric, cut:**
(4) 6½" (16.5 cm) squares

**From the backing fabric, cut:**
(1) 4¾" × 18½" (12 cm × 47 cm) strip

(1) 16¼" × 18½" (41 cm × 47 cm) rectangle

**From the binding fabric, cut:**
(2) 2½" (6.5 cm) × WOF strips

### author advice

#### MAKE A FOUR-BLOCK OPPOSITES ATTRACT PILLOW

To make an Opposites Attract Pillow with 4 Nine Patch blocks, you will need the same amount of fabric as listed in the Materials list. Cut out (5) 6½" (16.5 cm) background fabric squares instead of 4, then make 4 Nine Patch blocks instead of 5. Arrange the Nine Patch blocks and background fabric squares as shown, then follow steps 5–9 to complete the pillow.

## MAKING THE BLOCKS

For detailed directions, see How to Make a Two-Color Nine Patch Block at the beginning of Chapter Two.

**1** Arrange the fabric print strips in sets of 3, then sew the strips together along the long edges (**Figure 1**).

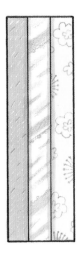

FIGURE 1

**2** Using a rotary cutter, cut each strip set into (5) 2½" (6.5 cm) wide units and arrange as shown (**Figure 2**).

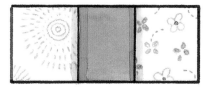

FIGURE 2

**3** Sew the rows together to make a Nine Patch block (**Figure 3**). The current block size is 6½" (16.5 cm) square. Make 5 blocks.

FIGURE 3

## ASSEMBLING THE PILLOW

**4** Arrange the Nine Patch blocks and 6½" (16.5 cm) background fabric squares as shown (**Figure 4**).

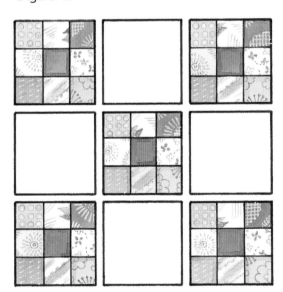

FIGURE 4

**5** Pin and sew the blocks together by row. Press toward the Nine Patch blocks. Pin and sew the rows together (**Figure 5**). Press toward the top and bottom rows.

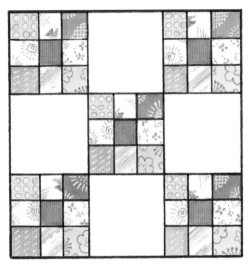

FIGURE 5

**6** Layer the batting and pillow top, and baste them together. Quilt as desired. (The featured pillow was machine-quilted by sewing cross-hatched lines along the diagonals through the Nine Patch blocks.)

**7** Attach the backing and zipper (see Making a Backing with a Zipper in *Chapter Ten*).

**8** Bind the pillow cover. Fill with the pillow insert.

*For tips and detailed instructions on how to finish your pillow, turn to Chapter Ten: Putting It All Together.*

# CHAPTER 3

# The Half-Square Triangle

Half-Square Triangles are the starting point for many designs. Some quilters use them on their own to create patterns, while others build on them to make different blocks. You can also rotate them to completely change the look of a block.

When making Half-Square Triangles, I prefer to make larger blocks, then trim them down to size using Bloc Loc Half Square Triangle Square Up rulers. While some quilters may see this as an extra step, I believe taking the extra time to do this actually saves time and frustration down the track. The points in your blocks will match up better and ensure your finished project looks better, too. I've also found that when Half-Square Triangles are made to size, you sometimes have to deal with bias stretch, which can distort the points when pressing and involve unpicking and sewing scant seams to make things fit. It takes less time to construct a project when everything lines up beautifully.

# How to Make a Half-Square Triangle

To make an HST (Half-Square Triangle), you will need two fabric squares that are the exact same size but cut from different fabrics.

*All seam allowances are ¼" (6 mm) unless otherwise noted.*

**1** Using a pencil, mark a diagonal line from corner to corner on the wrong side of the lighter fabric square. Place the other square and marked fabric square right sides together (**Figure 1**).

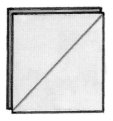

FIGURE 1          FIGURE 2

**2** Pin the squares together and sew along both sides of the marked line with a ¼" (6 mm) seam allowance (**Figure 2**).
**Tip:** *If you're making a number of blocks, see Chain-Piecing Half-Square Triangles to speed up the process.*

**3** Rotary cut along the diagonal line. Open both squares and press the seams toward the main or darker fabric. Makes 2 Half-Square Triangles (**Figure 3**).

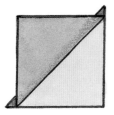 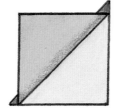

FIGURE 3

**4** Trim the Half-Square Triangles to the required size (**Figure 4**).

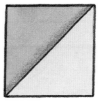 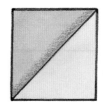

FIGURE 4

## author advice

### CHAIN-PIECING HALF-SQUARE TRIANGLES

Chain-piecing blocks lets you make a lot of blocks more quickly. I especially like using this method for blocks that will be trimmed down later. Another perk is that you don't have to stop and start to backstitch the seams.

To chain-piece Half-Square Triangles, mark and pair up all of your squares as described in steps 1 and 2. Feed the first pair of squares through your sewing machine. Once you've stitched past the first pair, feed the next pair through your machine. Continue sewing this way until all of the pairs are sewn together. When you're done, snip the thread between the pairs.

# In the Middle Mini Quilt

Once you know how to make Half-Square Triangles, it's easy to make other blocks such as a Churn Dash. The sleek lines of this quilt look great in a simple two-color combination with a variety of prints in the colorways. Mix it up with any color combination you like.

## MATERIALS

Gray prints, 4 fat eighths (each 9" × 21" [23 cm × 53.5 cm]) (fabrics A, B, C, D)

Aqua/gray prints, 4 fat eighths (each 9" × 21" [23 cm × 53.5 cm]) (fabrics E, F, G, H)

Gray dot background fabric, ½ yard (0.5 m)

Backing fabric, 30" (76 cm) square

Binding fabric, ¼ yard (0.2 m)

Batting, 30" (76 cm) square

Half Square Triangle Square Up Ruler, 2½" (6.5 cm) (optional)

**Finished Size:**
22½" (57 cm) square

**Finished Block Size:**
2" (5 cm) square

**FAT-EIGHTH FRIENDLY**

*All seam allowances are ¼" (6 mm) unless otherwise noted.*

## CUTTING INSTRUCTIONS

**From two of the gray prints (fabrics A and B), cut:**
(5) 3" (7.5 cm) squares

(1) 2½" (6.5 cm) × WOF (width-of-fabric) strip; subcut into (8) 1½" × 2½" (3.8 cm × 6.5 cm) rectangles

**From two of the gray prints (fabrics C and D), cut:**
(6) 3" (7.5 cm) squares

(1) 2½" (6.5 cm) × WOF strip; subcut into (8) 1½" × 2½" (3.8 cm × 6.5 cm) rectangles

**From each of the aqua/gray prints (fabrics E, F, G, and H), cut:**
(4) 3" (7.5 cm) squares

(4) 1½" × 2½" (3.8 cm × 6.5 cm) rectangles

**From the gray dot background fabric, cut:**
(2) 3" (7.5 cm) × WOF strips; subcut into (14) 3" (7.5 cm) squares

(2) 2½" (6.5 cm) × WOF strips; subcut into (37) 2½" (6.5 cm) squares

(2) 2½" (6.5 cm) × WOF strips; subcut into (48) 1½" × 2½" (3.8 cm × 6.5 cm) rectangles

**From the binding fabric, cut:**
(3) 2½" (6.5 cm) × WOF strips

## MAKING THE BLOCKS

For detailed directions, see How to Make a Half-Square Triangle at the beginning of Chapter Three.

**1** Gather 3 fabric A squares, 3 fabric B squares, 2 fabric C squares, 2 fabric D squares, and (10) 3" (7.5 cm) gray dot background squares. Make 20 Half-Square Triangles by pairing each gray print square with a gray dot background fabric square (**Figure 1**). Trim the units to 2½" (6.5 cm) square.

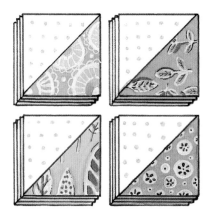

FIGURE 1

**2** Make a set of Half-Square Triangles by pairing (1) 3" (7.5 cm) square of fabric E, F, G, and H with (1) 3" (7.5 cm) gray dot background fabric square (**Figure 2**). Discard the second Half-Square Triangle from each combination pair. Trim the 4 blocks to 2½" (6.5 cm) square.

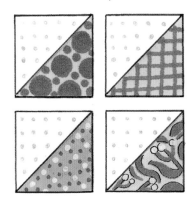

FIGURE 2

**3** Make another set of Half-Square Triangles with the following combinations (**Figure 3**):

(3) 3" (7.5 cm) fabric E squares with 1 each of fabrics A, C, and D

(3) 3" (7.5 cm) fabric F squares with 1 each of fabrics B, C, and D

(3) 3" (7.5 cm) fabric G squares with 1 each of fabrics B, C, and D

(3) 3" (7.5 cm) fabric H squares with 1 each of fabrics A, C, and D

Discard the second Half-Square Triangle from each combination pair. Trim the 12 blocks to 2½" (6.5 cm) square.

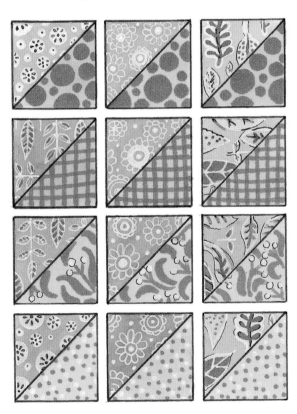

FIGURE 3

**4** Sew each of the 1½" × 2½" (3.8 cm × 6.5 cm) gray print rectangles to a 1½" × 2½" (3.8 cm × 6.5 cm) gray dot background rectangle along one long edge (**Figure 4**), pressing the seams toward the gray print fabric. Make 32 total.

FIGURE 4

**5** Sew each of the 1½" × 2½" (3.8 cm × 6.5 cm) aqua/gray print rectangles to a 1½" × 2½" (3.8 cm × 6.5 cm) gray dot background rectangle along one long edge (**Figure 5**). Press the seams toward the aqua/gray fabric. Make 16 total.

FIGURE 5

## ASSEMBLING THE QUILT

**6** Arrange the Half-Square Triangles, pieced rectangle blocks, and (37) 2½" (6.5 cm) background squares as shown (**Figure 6**).

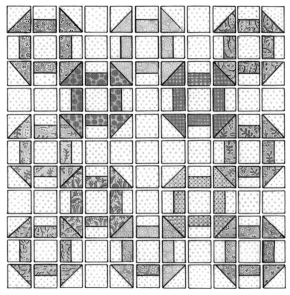

FIGURE 6

**7** Pin and sew the blocks in the first row together (**Figure 7**), pressing the seams open. Continue pinning and sewing the blocks together by row.

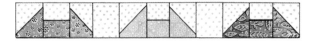

FIGURE 7

**8** Pin and sew the rows together, making sure to pin where the seams meet for accurate piecing (**Figure 8**). Press the seams open.

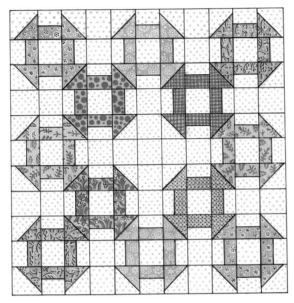

FIGURE 8

**9** Layer the backing (wrong-side up), the batting, and the quilt top (right-side up), and baste them together. Quilt as desired. (The featured quilt was machine-quilted by sewing diagonal lines through the center of the aqua/gray blocks and large cross-hatched lines through the outside blocks.)

**10** Bind the quilt.

*For tips and detailed instructions on how to finish your quilt, turn to Chapter Ten: Putting It All Together.*

# Hearts on Fire Quilt

Half-Square Triangles are one of my favorite blocks to piece. They are striking on their own and can be used to make different pattern combinations by simply rotating the block. I always trim my Half-Square Triangles. This is an important step to ensure all of your points meet and you have a quilt top that you are happy with in the end. I used a directional layout for the blocks in this quilt, but you can turn them any way you please.

## MATERIALS

Assorted prints*, (15) 1/6 yard (15 cm) cuts

Chambray background fabric, 2 1/4 yards (2.1 m)

Backing fabric, 4 yards (3.7 m)

Binding fabric, 5/8 yard (0.6 m)

Batting, 68" (172.5 cm) square

Half Square Triangle Square Up Ruler, 4 1/2" (11.5 cm) (optional)

*This quilt includes 5 red, 5 blue, and 5 neutral prints.

**Finished Size:**
60 1/2" (153.5) square

**Finished Block Size:**
3 1/2" (9 cm) square

*All seam allowances are ¼" (6 mm) unless otherwise noted.*

## CUTTING INSTRUCTIONS

**From each of the 15 assorted prints, cut:**
(6) 4½" (11.5 cm) squares (90 total)

**From the chambray background fabric, cut:**
(2) 4½" (11.5 cm) × WOF (width-of-fabric) strips; subcut into (10) 4½" (11.5 cm) squares

(4) 4" (10 cm) × WOF strips; subcut into (4) 4" (10 cm) squares

(3) 4" × 7½" (10 cm × 19 cm) strips

(2) 4" × 11" (10 cm × 28 cm) strips

(2) 4" × 14½" (10 cm × 37 cm) strips

(2) 4" × 18" (10 cm × 45.5 cm) strips

**From the remaining length of chambray, cut:**
(2) 9½" × 39" (24 cm × 99 cm) strips for the side borders

(2) 11½" × 60½" (29 cm × 153.5 cm) strips for the top and bottom border

**From the binding fabric, cut:**
(7) 2½" (6.5 cm) × WOF strips

## MAKING THE BLOCKS

For detailed directions, see How to Make a Half-Square Triangle at the beginning of Chapter Three.

**1** Make 20 Half-Square Triangles using (10) 4½" (11.5 cm) chambray squares and (10) 4½" (11.5 cm) assorted prints (**Figure 1**). Trim the blocks to 4" (10 cm) square. These are the outside of the heart.

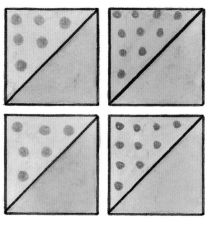

FIGURE 1

**2** Make 78 Half-Square Triangles with the remaining 4½" (11.5 cm) assorted prints (**Figure 2**). Trim the blocks to 4" (10 cm) square.

FIGURE 2

## ASSEMBLING THE QUILT

**3** Referring to **Figure 3**, arrange the chambray/assorted prints and the assorted prints Half-Square Triangles as shown.

**Note:** *The blocks within the heart shape are turned so they echo the shape of the heart.*

Then arrange the chambray squares and strips as follows:

Rows 1 and 7: Place the 4" (10 cm) squares in the corners.

Rows 1 and 8: Place the 4" × 7½" (10 cm × 19 cm) strips in the middle of Row 1 and at the sides of Row 8.

Rows 9–11: Place the 4" × 11" (10 cm × 28 cm) strips on both sides of Row 9, the 4" × 14½" (10 cm × 37 cm) strips on both sides of Row 10, and the 4" × 18" (10 cm × 45.5 cm) strips on both sides of Row 11.

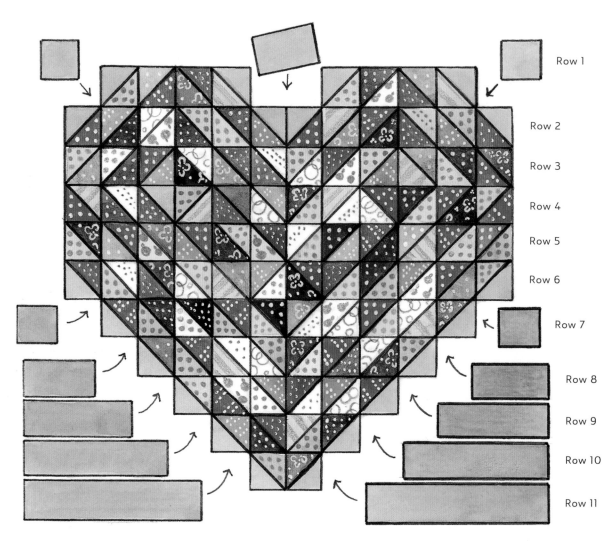

FIGURE 3

**4** Pin and sew the blocks together in each row, pressing seams to the left for odd rows and to the right for even rows to nest the seams (**Figure 4**).

FIGURE 4

**5** Sew the rows together, matching the seams for a neat finish (**Figure 5**). Press the seams open. The finished center heart should measure 39" × 42½" (99 cm × 108 cm).

FIGURE 5

**6** Referring to **Figure 6**, pin the left and right border strips to the sides of the quilt top, making sure the border measurements match the sides of the quilt center. Sew the border strips to the quilt and press the seams open. Then pin and sew the top and bottom border strips to your quilt top, making sure the measurements match the quilt top. Press the seams open.

**Note:** *Sometimes the sides can become stretched, so measure twice through the center of the quilt top (but not the edges), then average the results to make sure your border measurement is correct.*

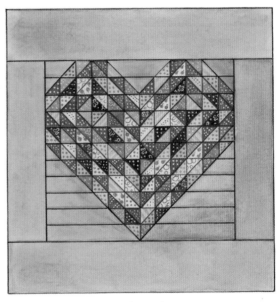

FIGURE 6

**7** Layer the backing (wrong-side up), the batting, and the quilt top (right-side up), and baste them together. Quilt as desired. (The featured quilt was professionally longarm quilted.)

**8** Bind the quilt.

*For tips and detailed instructions on how to finish your quilt, turn to Chapter Ten: Putting It All Together.*

# CHAPTER 4

# Flying Geese

Flying Geese are traditional blocks that can be used to create stunning modern patterns. Made using two prints or colors, Flying Geese can be used on their own, as in the Duck, Duck, Goose Mini Quilt, or combined with other blocks to create a whole new pattern, such as the stars in the Star-Filled Skies Quilt.

Flying Geese blocks are most effective with a simple color palette, and they also make a fantastic scrap-buster block. They create movement in quilts, and by simply changing the direction of the blocks, you can make interesting patterns and new designs .

# How to Make a Flying Geese Block

To make a Flying Geese block, you will need a fabric rectangle, two matching fabric squares that are the exact same size, an erasable fabric marker, and a Flying Geese Square Up Ruler (optional).

## author advice

### PRESS WITH CARE

Take care when pressing Flying Geese blocks. The seams are sewn on the bias (diagonal of the fabric) and can easily stretch. Be sure to press seams gently. You may also find it helpful to use a spray starch to help keep seams nice and straight.

*All seam allowances are ¼" (6 mm) unless otherwise noted.*

**1** Using the erasable fabric marker, draw a diagonal line from corner to corner on the wrong side of both squares. Place the first square on the right half of the rectangle (line going from upper left to lower right) with right sides together and edges aligned as shown. Pin the pieces together, then sew along the marked diagonal line (**Figure 1**).

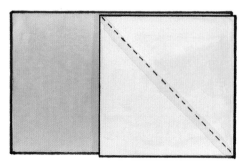

FIGURE 1

**2** Trim the excess fabric as shown, leaving a ¼" (6 mm) seam allowance (**Figure 2**).

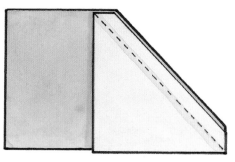

FIGURE 2

**3** Press the seam toward the background fabric (**Figure 3**).

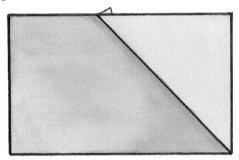

FIGURE 3

**4** Repeat steps 1–3 for the second square on the left side of the Flying Geese block. Be sure to orient the square so the diagonal seams cross at the top center of the block (**Figure 4**).

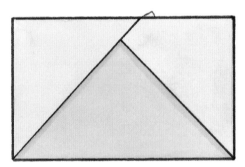

FIGURE 4

**5** Trim the block to the desired size.

# Duck, Duck, Goose Mini Quilt

Made with Flying Geese blocks, this mini quilt uses just two main colors to let your fabrics shine. I like to use the Bloc Loc Flying Geese Square Up Ruler (1½" × 3" [3.8 cm × 7.5 cm]) when making this block for perfect points every time. Although there is the extra step of trimming the blocks with this ruler, it is well worth the effort for a better finish to your project.

## MATERIALS

Red print fabric, ³/8 yard (0.3 m)

Blue print fabric, ³/8 yard (0.3 m)

Background and border fabric, ⁷/8 yard (0.8 m)

Backing fabric, ⁷/8 yard (0.8 m)

Binding fabric, ¼ yard (0.2 m)

Batting, 32" (81.5 m)

Erasable marking pen or fabric pencil

Flying Geese Square Up Ruler, 1½" × 3" (3.8 cm × 7.5 cm) (optional)

**Finished Size:**
24½" (62 cm) square

**Finished Block Size:**
3" (7.5 cm) square

**SCRAP FRIENDLY**

*All seam allowances are ¼" (6 mm) unless otherwise noted.*

## CUTTING INSTRUCTIONS

**From the red print fabric, cut:**
(2) 2¼" (5.5 cm) × WOF (width-of-fabric) strips; subcut into (21) 2¼" × 3¾" (5.5 cm × 9.5 cm) rectangles

(3) 2¼" (5.5 cm) × WOF strips; subcut into (42) 2¼" (5.5 cm) squares

**From the blue print fabric, cut**
(2) 2¼" (5.5 cm) × WOF strips; subcut into (21) 2¼" × 3¾" (5.5 cm × 9.5 cm) rectangles

(3) 2¼" (5.5 cm) × WOF strips; subcut into (42) 2¼" (5.5 cm) squares

**From the background fabric, cut:**
(4) 2¼" (5.5 cm) × WOF stips; subcut into (42) 2¼" × 3¾" (5.5 cm × 9.5 cm) rectangles

(5) 2¼" (5.5 cm) × WOF strips; subcut into (84) 2¼" (5.5 cm) squares

(2) 3½" (9 cm) × WOF strips; subcut into the following strip lengths for borders:
(4) 3½" × 6½" (9 cm × 16.5 cm)
(2) 3½" × 9½" (9 cm × 24 cm)
(2) 3½" × 12½" (9 cm × 31.5 cm)

**From the binding fabric, cut:**
(3) 2½" (6.5 cm) × WOF strips

## MAKING THE BLOCKS

For detailed directions, see How to Make a Flying Geese Block at the beginning of Chapter Four.
**Note:** *Each completed quilt block is made with 1 print Flying Geese block and 1 reverse print Flying Geese block.*

**1** Make a reverse print Flying Geese unit using (1) 2¼" × 3¾" (5.5 cm × 9.5 cm) background fabric rectangle and (2) 2¼" (5.5 cm) red print squares (**Figure 1**). Trim the excess fabric from the triangles down to ¼" (6 mm) seam allowance. Then trim the completed unit to 2" × 3½" (5 cm × 9 cm). Press the seams toward the background fabric. Make 21 units.

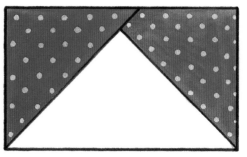

FIGURE 1

**2** Make a print Flying Geese unit with (1) 2¼" × 3¾" (5.5 cm × 9.5 cm) red print rectangle and (2) 2¼" (5.5 cm) background squares (**Figure 2**). Trim the excess fabric from the triangles down to ¼" (6 mm) seam allowance. Then trim the completed unit to 2" × 3½" (5 cm × 9 cm). Press the seams toward the background fabric. Make 21 units.

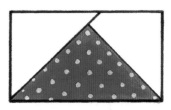

FIGURE 2

**3** Referring to **Figure 3**, pin together 1 red print Flying Geese unit and 1 reverse red print Flying Geese unit with the Geese "flying" in the same direction. Sew the units together to complete 1 red Flying Geese block. The block should measure 3½" (9 cm) square. Press the seams toward the red print Flying Geese fabric. Make 21 red Flying Geese blocks.

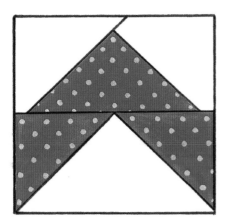

FIGURE 3

**4** Following steps 1–3, make 21 blue print Flying Geese units and 21 reverse blue print Flying Geese units. Pin and sew together 1 blue Flying Geese unit and 1 reverse blue Flying Geese unit with the Geese "flying" in the same direction to make a blue Flying Geese quilt block. Make 21 blue Flying Geese blocks.

## ASSEMBLING THE QUILT

**5** Referring to **Figure 4**, arrange 36 of the completed Flying Geese blocks in 6 rows of 6 blocks, alternating the block colors and directions as shown. (For the center of the quilt shown here, the blocks are positioned so the Flying Geese units in each color are pointing in the same direction.) Sew the blocks together by row, pinning as you go and pressing the seams open. Sew the rows together, pressing the seams open. The center should measure 18½" (47 cm) square.

FIGURE 4

**6** To make the right border, sew the short end of (1) 3½" × 6½" (9 cm × 16.5 cm) background strip to 1 blue Flying Geese block (flying up). Sew (1) 3½" × 9½" (9 cm × 24 cm) background strip to the opposite side of the block to finish the border (**Figure 5**). For the left border, sew the short end of (1) 3½" × 6½" (9 cm × 16.5 cm) background strip below a red Flying Geese block (flying left). Then sew (1) 3½" × 9½" (9 cm × 24 cm) background strip to the top of the block to finish the border. Press the seams toward the border. Pin and sew the left and right borders to the quilt center.

**7** Using **Figure 6** as a guide, make the top and bottom borders. Sew together in this order (1) 3½" × 6½" (9 cm × 16.5 cm) background strip, 1 red Flying Geese unit (flying left), 1 blue Flying Geese block (flying up), and (1) 3½" × 12½" (9 cm × 31.5 cm) background strip. Pin and sew the border in place along the top of the quilt center. Press the seams toward the border. Make a bottom border with the remaining background strips and Flying Geese blocks (orient the Flying Geese as shown), then pin and sew the border in place along the bottom of the quilt center.

FIGURE 6

**8** Layer the backing (wrong-side up), the batting, and the quilt top (right-side up), and baste them together. Quilt as desired. (The featured quilt was machine-quilted by sewing horizontal and vertical lines along the seam lines about ¼" [6 mm] from the stitching.)

**9** Bind the quilt.

*For tips and detailed instructions on how to finish your quilt, turn to Chapter Ten: Putting It All Together.*

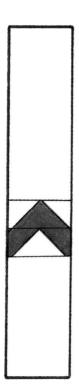

FIGURE 5

# Star-Filled Skies Quilt

Once you've mastered making Flying Geese blocks, you can create lots of different designs. Turning Flying Geese blocks into Star blocks as shown here is one example—and lets you show just how creative you can be.

## MATERIALS

Pink print fabric, 5 fat quarters
(each 18" × 21" [45.5 cm x 53.5 cm])

Blue print fabric, 5 fat eighths
(each 9" × 21" [23 cm × 53.5 cm])

Green print fabric, 5 fat eighths
(each 9" × 21" [23 cm × 53.5 cm])

Mini-dot background fabric, 3¼ yards (3 m)

Backing fabric, 3¼ yards (3 m)

Binding fabric, ½ yard (0.5 m)

Batting, 56" × 68" (142 cm × 172.5 cm)

Erasable marking pen or fabric pencil

Flying Geese Square Up Rulers (optional)*:
    ¾" × 1½" (2 cm × 3.8 cm)
    1½" × 3" (3.8 cm × 7.5 cm)
    3" × 6" (7.5 cm × 15 cm) (optional)

*I like to use Bloc Loc Flying Geese Square Up Rulers for the Star blocks because they help me achieve perfect points every time.*

**Finished Size:**
48½" × 60½" (123 cm × 153.5 cm)

**Finished Block Size:**
12" (30.5) square

*All seam allowances are ¼" (6 mm) unless otherwise noted.*

## CUTTING INSTRUCTIONS

**From each of the pink print fabrics, cut:**

(1) 6½" (16.5 cm) center square

(8) 3¾" (9.5 cm) squares

**From each of the blue print fabrics, cut:**

(2) 3½" (9 cm) center squares

(16) 2¼" (5.5 cm) squares

**From each of the green print fabrics, cut:**

(5) 2" (5 cm) center squares

(40) 1½" (3.8 cm) squares

**From the background fabric, cut:**

(4) 1¼" (3.2 cm) × WOF (width-of-fabric) strips; subcut into (100) 1¼" (3.2 cm) corner squares for green Star blocks

(4) 2¼" (5.5 cm) × WOF strips; subcut into (100) 1½" × 2¼" (3.8 cm × 5.5 cm) rectangles for green Flying Geese backgrounds

(2) 2" (5 cm) × WOF strips; subcut into (40) 2" (5 cm) corner squares for blue Star blocks

(3) 3¾" (9.5 cm) × WOF strips; subcut into (40) 2¼" × 3¾" (5.5 cm × 9.5 cm) rectangles for blue Flying Geese backgrounds

(2) 3½" (9 cm) × WOF strips; subcut into (20) 3½" (9 cm) corner squares for the pink Star blocks

(2) 6¾" (17 cm) × WOF strips; subcut into (20) 3¾" × 6¾" (9.5 cm × 17 cm) rectangles for pink Flying Geese backgrounds

(2) 3½" (9 cm) × WOF strips; subcut into (21) 3½" (9 cm) squares (9 for block A and 12 for block B)

(8) 6½" (16.5 cm) × WOF strips; subcut into:

  (6) 3½" × 6½" (9 cm × 16.5 cm) rectangles for block B

  (15) 6½" (16.5 cm) squares (9 for block A and 6 for block B)

  (15) 6½" × 9½" (16.5 cm × 24 cm) rectangles (9 for block A and 6 for block B)

**From the binding fabric, cut:**

(6) 2½" (6.5 cm) × WOF strips

## MAKING THE BLOCKS

For detailed directions, see How to Make A Flying Geese Block at the beginning of Chapter Four.

**Note:** *To make this quilt, you will need (21) 3½" (9 cm) green Star blocks, (9) 6½" (16.5 cm) blue Star blocks, and (5) 12½" (31.5 cm) pink Star blocks. You will have spare blue and green blocks, so you can play with the arrangement. When the quilt top is complete, you can use the leftover blocks to create a matching pillow or incorporate them into a pieced backing.*

**1** Make a green Flying Geese unit with (2) 1½" (3.8 cm) green squares and (1) 1½" × 2¼" (3.8 cm × 5.5 cm) background fabric rectangle. Trim the excess fabric from the triangles to ¼" (6 mm) seam allowance. Square up (or trim) the unit to 1¼" × 2" (3.2 cm × 5 cm) (**Figure 1**). Make 20 Flying Geese units from each of the 5 green prints (100 total).

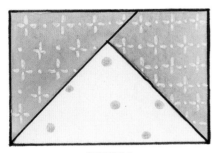

FIGURE 1

**2** To make a green Star unit, sew (1) 1¼" (3.2 cm) corner square to both sides of a green Flying Geese unit (**Figure 2**). Press the seams open. Make 2 units (**Figure 3**). Sew 2 Flying Geese units to both sides of a green 2" (5 cm) center square (**Figure 4**). Press the seams toward the center. Sew the 2 Flying Geese rows to the top and bottom of the center block row (**Figure 5**). Press the seams open. The finished green Star unit should measure 3½" (9 cm) (**Figure 6**). Make 25 green Star units.

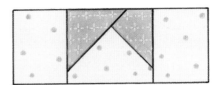

FIGURE 2

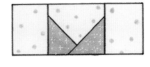

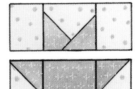

FIGURE 3

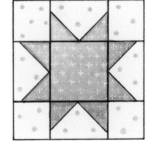

FIGURE 4

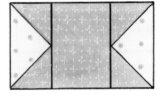

FIGURE 5

FIGURE 6

**3** Following steps 1 and 2, make 10 blue Star units and 5 pink Star units.
**Note:** *Square up (or trim) the 40 blue Flying Geese units to 2" × 3½" (5 cm × 9 cm) and the 20 pink Flying Geese units to 3½" × 6½" (9 cm × 16.5 cm). Set the units aside.*

**4** Using **Figure 7** as a guide, make block A. Sew (1) 6½" (16.5 cm) background square to 1 side of a blue Star unit, pressing the seam toward the background fabric (**Figure 8**). Sew (1) 3½" (9 cm) background square to one side of a green Star unit, pressing the seam toward the background fabric (**Figure 9**). Sew the green Star unit to the 6½" × 9½" (16.5 cm × 24 cm) rectangle (**Figure 10**). Then sew the green Star unit and blue Star unit together, pressing the seams open (**Figure 11**). Make 9 of block A.

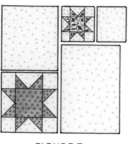

FIGURE 7

FIGURE 8

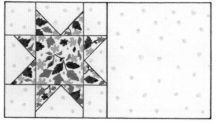

FIGURE 9

FIGURE 10

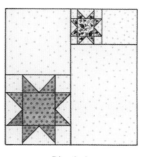

Block A

FIGURE 11

**5** Using **Figure 12** as a guide, make block B. Sew (1) 3½" (9 cm) background square to 1 side of a green Star unit, pressing the seam toward the background fabric. Make 2 green Star units (**Figure 13**). Sew a 3½" × 6½" (9 cm × 16.5 cm) background rectangle to 1 of the green Star units, pressing the seam toward the background fabric (**Figure 14**). Sew a 6½" (16.5 cm) background square to the left side (make sure the Star is in the middle) and press the seam toward the background fabric. Sew the 6½" × 9½" (16.5 cm × 24 cm) background rectangle to the side of the other green Star unit, pressing the seam toward the background fabric (**Figure 15**). Sew the two green Star block units together and press the seams open (**Figure 16**). Make 6 of block B.

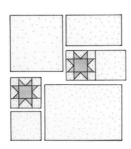

FIGURE 12

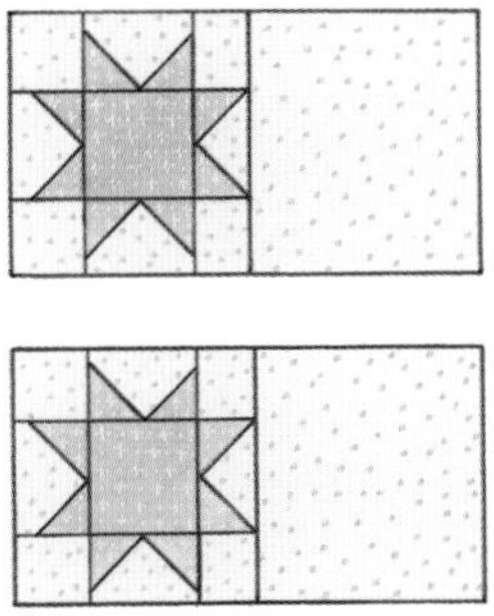

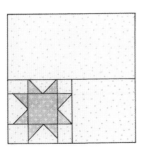

FIGURE 14

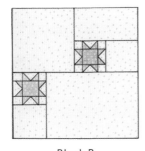

Block B

FIGURE 16

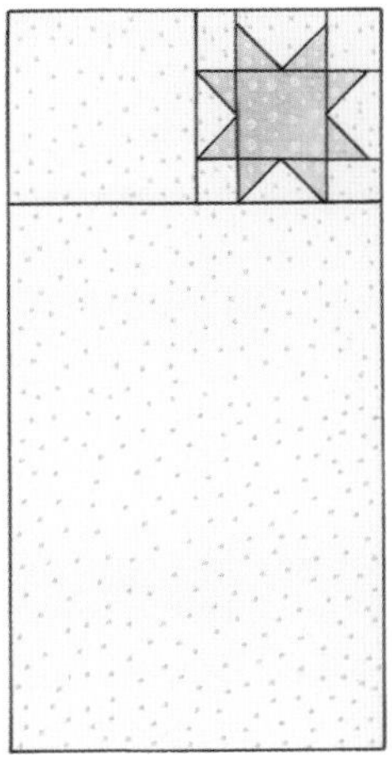

## ASSEMBLING THE QUILT

Refer to **Figure 17** throughout assembly.

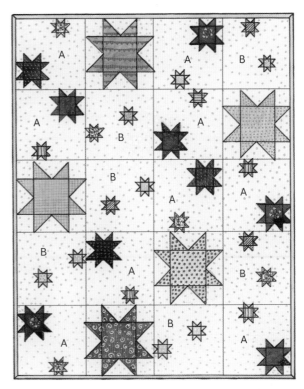

FIGURE 17

**6** Arrange the 5 pink Star units, 9 block A units, and 6 block B units in 5 rows with 4 blocks in each row as shown or play with the arrangement to create your own design.

**7** Pin and sew the blocks together by row, pressing the seams to the right for even rows and to the left for odd rows. Sew the rows together, pressing all of the seams open.

**8** Layer the backing (wrong-side up), the batting, and the quilt top (right-side up), then baste them together. Quilt as desired. (The featured quilt was professionally longarm quilted.)

**9** Bind the quilt.

*For tips and detailed instructions on how to finish your quilt, turn to Chapter Ten: Putting It All Together.*

FIGURE 13

FIGURE 15

# CHAPTER 5

# The Pinwheel

Once you have mastered making Half-Square Triangles, you're ready to try making Pinwheel blocks. These fun and whimsical blocks will build on your skill set and let you add new designs to create many more quilts and projects, including the Spinning Tops Quilt and Summer Breeze Table Runner in this chapter.

These projects allow you to use fabric bundles. I love coordinating fabrics specifically for the person I am creating the project for. The Spinning Tops Quilt is a great design that would suit anybody—from a child to an adult—and really showcases fabrics. The Summer Breeze Table Runner would make a lovely handmade gift that can be customized to match any décor. Both of these projects are also great for using up fabric scraps.

# How to Make a Pinwheel Block

For each Pinwheel block, you will need four fabric squares—two main and two background—that are all the exact same size. You will also need an erasable fabric marker.

*All seam allowances are ¼" (6 mm) unless otherwise noted.*

**1** Using an erasable fabric marker, draw a diagonal line from corner to corner on the wrong side of one of the main squares. Place the marked main square and background fabric square right sides together. Pin the squares together, then sew along both sides of the marked line with a ¼" (6 mm) seam allowance (**Figure 1**).

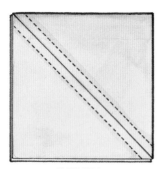

FIGURE 1

**2** Rotary cut the block in half along the marked line (**Figure 2**).

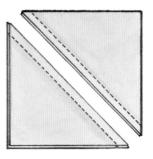

FIGURE 2

**3** Press the seams toward the darker fabric, then trim both blocks to the desired size (**Figure 3**). This makes 2 Half-Square Triangle units.

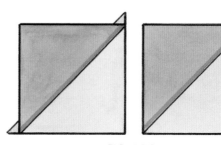

FIGURE 3

**4** Repeat steps 1–3 with another background square and a main fabric square to make a second set of Half-Square Triangle units.

**5** Arrange the 4 Half-Square Triangle units as shown, rotating each 90 degrees so the darker fabric appears to rotate around the Pinwheel block (**Figure 4**).

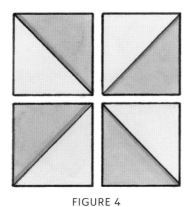

FIGURE 4

**6** Pin and sew the Half-Square Triangle units on the top row together, then press the seam toward the darker fabric. Repeat for the bottom row.

**7** Pin and sew the 2 rows together (**Figure 5**). Press the seam open.
**Note:** *The seams should "nest." Because you pressed the seams toward the darker fabric, they will fall in opposite directions when placed right sides together, which helps distribute the bulk.*

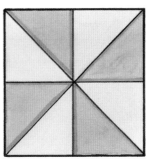

FIGURE 5

# Spinning Tops Quilt

Pinwheel blocks are easy to make, and you can create amazing designs simply by turning finished Half-Square Triangles in different directions. This eye-catching design showcases the beautiful simplicity of Pinwheel blocks.

## MATERIALS

Assorted prints, 10 fat eighths
(each 9" × 21" [23 cm × 53.5 cm])

White background fabric, 3½ yards (3.2 m)

Backing fabric, 3⅞ yards (3.5 m)

Binding fabric, ½ yard (0.5 m)

Batting, 68" (172.5 cm) square

Half Square Triangle Square Up Ruler, 2½"
(6.5 cm) (optional)

**Finished Size:**
60½" (153.5 cm) square

**Finished Block Size:**
5" (12.5 cm) square

**FAT-EIGHTH FRIENDLY**

*All seam allowances are ¼" (6 mm) unless otherwise noted.*

## CUTTING INSTRUCTIONS

**From each of the 10 assorted prints, cut:**
(10) 3½" (9 cm) squares (100 total)

**From the background fabric, cut:**
(9) 3½" (9 cm) × WOF (width-of-fabric) strips; subcut into (100) 3½" (9 cm) squares

(16) 5½" (14 cm) × WOF strips; subcut into:

(10) 5½" (14 cm) squares for Piece 1

(9) 5½" × 10½" (14 cm × 26.5 cm) strips for Piece 2

(8) 5½" × 15½" (14 cm × 39.5 cm) strips for Piece 3

(3) 5½" × 20½" (14 cm × 52 cm) strips for Piece 4

(5) 5½" × 30½" (14 cm × 77.5 cm) strips for Piece 5

**From the binding fabric, cut:**
(7) 2½" (6.5 cm) × WOF strips

## MAKING THE BLOCKS

For detailed directions, see How to Make a Pinwheel Block at the beginning of Chapter Five.

**1** Make 200 Half-Square Triangle units with the 3½" (9 cm) print squares and 3½" (9 cm) background fabric squares. Trim each Half-Square Triangle unit to 3" (7.5 cm) square. To construct each Pinwheel block, sew together 4 matching Half-Square Triangle units as shown (**Figure 1**). The Pinwheel blocks should measure 5½" (14 cm) square. Make 50 Pinwheel blocks total. Set the blocks aside.

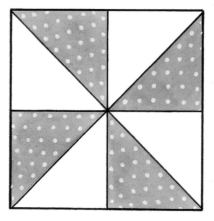

FIGURE 1

author advice

**PINWHEEL PLACEMENT**

Take your time with the arrangement so you have a balanced color placement in your quilt top.

## ASSEMBLING THE QUILT

**2** Referring to **Figure 2**, arrange the Pinwheel blocks and Pieces 1–5 in horizontal rows as shown, or as desired.

**3** Pin and sew the blocks and pieces together by row, pressing the seams open. Pin and sew the rows together, matching the Spinning Top seams where needed for a neat finish. Press the seams open.

**4** Layer the backing (wrong-side up), the batting, and the quilt top (right-side up), and baste them together. Quilt as desired. (The featured quilt was professionally longarm quilted in an allover design.)

**5** Bind the quilt.

*For tips and detailed instructions on how to finish your quilt, turn to Chapter Ten: Putting It All Together.*

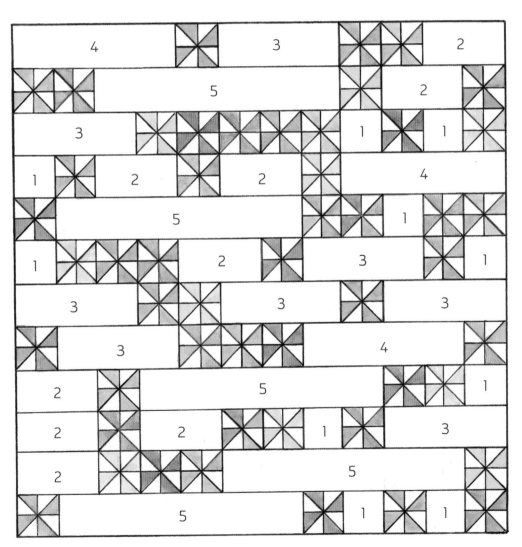

FIGURE 2

# Summer Breeze
# Table Runner

Turn sweet Pinwheel blocks into a beautiful runner that appears to blow in the summer breeze. This fanciful design makes a stunning centerpiece for any celebration with family and friends.

## MATERIALS

Green print fabric, 4 fat eighths
(each 9" × 21" [23 cm × 53.5 cm])

Blue print fabrics, 4 fat eighths
(each 9" × 21" [23 cm × 53.5 cm])

White spot background fabric, 3/4 yard (0.7 m)

Backing fabric, 1½ yards (1.4 m)

Blue border and binding fabric, ½ yard (0.5 m)

Batting, 26" × 58" (66 cm × 147.5 cm)

Half Square Triangle Square Up Ruler, 2½"
(6.5 cm) (optional)

**Finished Size:**
18½" × 50½" (47 cm × 128.5 cm)

**Finished Block Size:**
4" (10 cm) square

**FAT-EIGHTH FRIENDLY**

*All seam allowances are ¼" (6 mm) unless otherwise noted.*

## CUTTING INSTRUCTIONS

**From 3 of the green prints, cut:**
(4) 3" (7.5 cm) squares (12 total)

**From the remaining green print, cut:**
(5) 3" (7.5 cm) squares

**From 3 of the blue prints, cut:**
(4) 3" (7.5 cm) squares (12 total)

**From the remaining blue print, cut:**
(5) 3" (7.5 cm) squares

**From the background fabric, cut:**
(3) 3" (7.5 cm) × WOF (width-of-fabric) strips; subcut into (34) 3" (7.5 cm) squares

(2) 4½" (11.5 cm) × WOF strips; subcut into (16) 4½" (11.5 cm) squares

(4) 2½" (6.5 cm) × WOF strips for the borders

**From the blue border and binding fabric, cut:**
(4) 1½" (3.8 cm) × WOF strips for the borders

(4) 2½" (6.5 cm) × WOF strips for the binding

## MAKING THE BLOCKS

For detailed directions, see How to Make a Pinwheel Block at the beginning of Chapter Five.

**1** Make 68 Half-Square Triangles with 17 each of the green and blue print 3" (7.5 cm) squares and (34) 3" (7.5 cm) background squares. Trim the Half-Square Triangle units to 2½" (6.5 cm) square.

**2** To construct each Pinwheel block, sew together 2 blue-and-white Half-Square Triangle units and 2 green-and-white Half-Square Triangle units as shown (**Figure 1**). The blocks should measure 4½" (11.5 cm) square. Make 17 Pinwheel blocks.

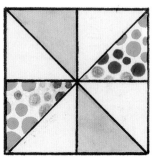

FIGURE 1

## ASSEMBLING THE RUNNER

**3** Arrange the Pinwheel blocks in rows, alternating 1 Pinwheel block and (1) 4½" (11.5 cm) background square (**Figure 2**). For this table runner, the blue prints are all facing in one direction, while the green prints are positioned in the opposite direction.

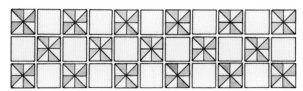

FIGURE 2

**4** Pin and sew the blocks in each row together, pressing the seams open (**Figure 3**).

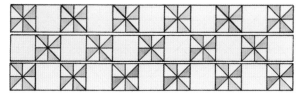

FIGURE 3

**5** Sew the rows together as shown to make the center of the runner (**Figure 4**). Press the seams open. The center should measure 12½" × 44½" (31.5 × 113 cm).

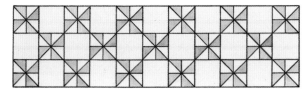

FIGURE 4

**6** Referring to **Figure 5**, cut 1 background strip in half. Sew each half to a full white border strip along the short ends. Press and cut each strip to measure 2½" × 48½" (6.5 cm × 123 cm) for the long side borders. Cut the remaining background strip into (2) 2½" × 12½" (6.5 cm × 31.5 cm) end border strips. Pin and sew 1 end border strip to each end of the table runner center. Press the seams open. Pin and sew the long side strips to both sides of the table runner center. Repeat this process for the blue borders, cutting the strips to 1½" × 16½" (3.8 cm × 42 cm) for the end borders and 1½" × 50½" (3.8 cm × 128.5 cm) for the long side borders (**Figure 6**). Press the seams open.

**7** Layer the backing (wrong-side up), the batting, and the quilt top (right-side up), and baste them together. Quilt the runner as desired. (The featured runner was machine-quilted by sewing diagonal lines through the center of the Pinwheel blocks.)

**8** Bind the table runner.

*For tips and detailed instructions on how to finish your table runner, turn to Chapter Ten: Putting It All Together.*

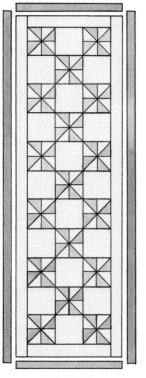

FIGURE 5

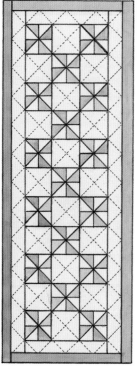

FIGURE 6

# CHAPTER 6

# Equilateral Triangles

Equilateral triangles are a simple way to add a bold element to any quilting project. Tackling triangles and points is easy with a few tips to make sure all of your points come together neatly and without bulk. These designs can be used on their own or to create additional blocks that increase the scope of the project.

Equilateral triangle rulers make sewing these blocks easier. They come with instructions for cutting and finished sizes. They also have the tip "cut off" so you don't have to deal with tricky points. I used a 60-degree equilateral triangle ruler for the Kite Tails Mini Quilt and the Pond Ripples Pillow projects in this chapter.

# How to Make Equilateral Triangles

You will need a main fabric, a background fabric, an equilateral triangle ruler, a rotary cutter, and pins.

*All seam allowances are 1⁄4" (6 mm) unless otherwise noted.*

**1** Cut the main and background fabrics into the required size strips for your project. Starting with the main fabric, line up the cutting size mark on an equilateral triangle ruler with the bottom of the strip, then cut the first triangle with a rotary cutter (**Figure 1**).

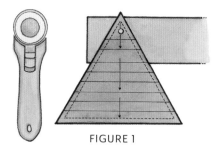

FIGURE 1

**2** Turn the ruler 180 degrees and cut the second triangle (**Figure 2**). Continue cutting triangles and turning the ruler around after each cut until you have the required number of triangles.

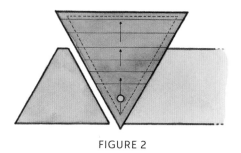

FIGURE 2

**3** In the same manner as steps 1 and 2, cut out the required number of equilateral triangles from the background fabric.

**4** Place 1 main fabric triangle and 1 background fabric triangle with right sides together and edges aligned. Place a pin in the side you plan to sew (**Figure 3**), then machine stitch down this side (**Figure 4**).

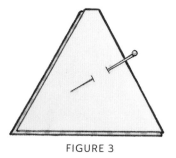

FIGURE 3

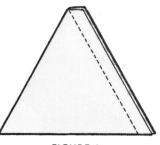

FIGURE 4

**5** Finger press the seam to the side (**Figure 5**).

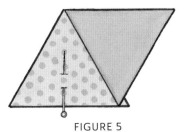

FIGURE 5

**6** Alternate triangle fabrics. Place the next triangle right-side down on top of the last sewn triangle (**Figure 6**). Sew the triangle in place (**Figure 7**), then finger press the seam to the side (**Figure 8**).

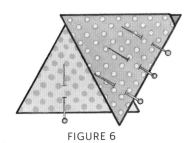

FIGURE 6

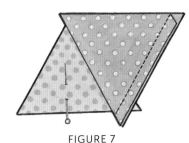

FIGURE 7

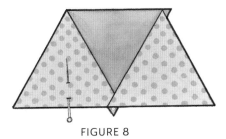

FIGURE 8

**7** Continue sewing the row with the required number of triangles in each. Press the completed row with an iron.

## author advice

### TIPS FOR BETTER TRIANGLES

- Place a pin in the first triangle, pointing up to indicate the top of the row, so you don't accidentally turn your row around as you sew and incorrectly sew them in the wrong direction (see **Figure 5**).

- Because you are sewing triangles on the bias (the stretch of the fabric), always pin the triangles in place when sewing so they do not stretch (see **Figure 6**).

- Use spray starch on sewn triangle seams when pressing to help ensure as little movement as possible.

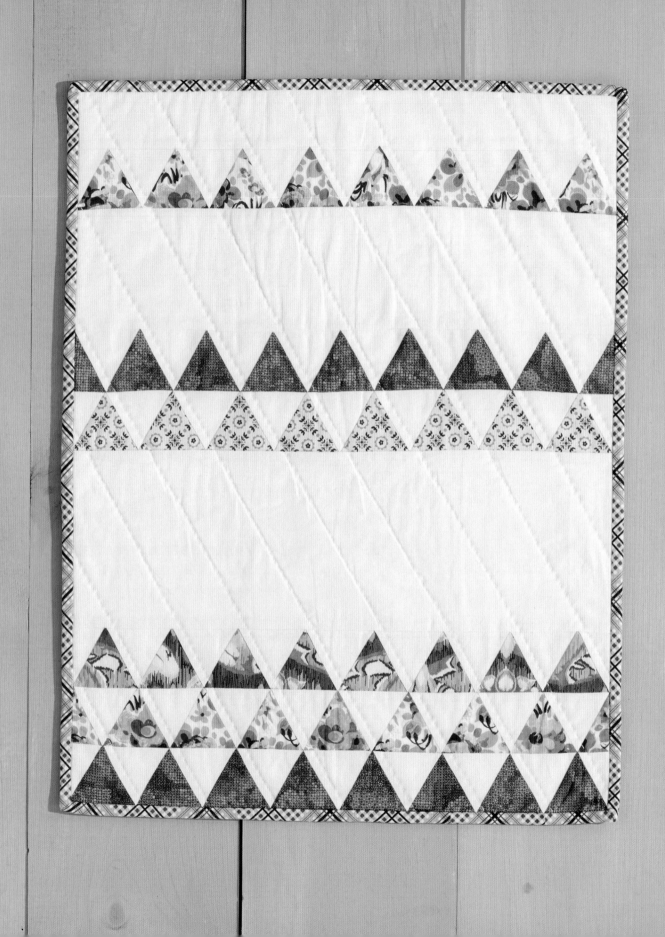

# Kite Tails
# Mini Quilt

As a child, I spent a lot of time flying kites with my siblings. When I was designing and making this mini quilt, the equilateral triangle shapes reminded me of the hours of fun I had and how the kite tails used to blow in the wind.

When using shapes that will be sewn on the bias, a few simple tricks will help you get beautiful points to your triangles. See Tips for Better Triangles at the beginning of this chapter.

**Finished Size:**
19" × 24½" (48.5 cm × 62 cm)

**FAT-EIGHTH FRIENDLY**

## MATERIALS

Blue/purple prints (fabrics A, B, C, and D), 4 fat eighths (each 9" × 21" [23 cm × 53.5 cm])

Linen background fabric, ⅝ yard (0.6 m) for rows and triangles

Backing fabric, ¾ yard (0.7 m)

Binding fabric, ¼ yard (0.2 m)

Batting, 27" × 33" (68.5 cm × 84 cm)

Handquilting thread

60-degree equilateral triangle ruler

*All seam allowances are ¼" (6 mm) unless otherwise noted.*

## CUTTING INSTRUCTIONS

**Note:** *If you're planning on rotary cutting with an equilateral triangle ruler that does not have clipped off tips, increase the width of the strips from 2½" (6.5 cm) to 2¾" (7 cm).*

**From fabric A, cut:**
(2) 2½" (6.5 cm) × WOF (width of fabric) strips; subcut into 17 triangles

**From fabric B, cut:**
(2) 2½" (6.5 cm) × WOF strips; subcut into 17 triangles

**From fabric C, cut:**
(1) 2½" (6.5 cm) × WOF strips; subcut into 8 triangles

**From fabric D, cut:**
(1) 2½" (6.5 cm) × WOF strips; subcut into 8 triangles

**From the background fabric, cut:**
(3) 2½" (6.5 cm) × WOF strips; subcut into (52) triangles

(1) 6½" × 19" (16.5 cm × 48.5 cm) rectangle

(1) 4½" × 19" (11.5 cm × 48.5 cm) rectangle

(1) 2½" × 19" (6.5 cm × 48.5 cm) rectangle

**From the binding fabric, cut:**
(3) 2½" (6.5 cm) × WOF strips

## MAKING THE ROWS

For detailed directions, see How to Make Equilateral Triangles at the beginning of Chapter Six.
**Note:** *Make sure each row starts with the triangle in the opposite direction of the previous row.*

**1** To make the first row, sew 9 background triangles and 8 fabric A triangles together top to bottom, starting with a background triangle (**Figure 1**).

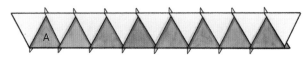

FIGURE 1

**2** To make the second row, sew 8 background triangles and 9 fabric B triangles together top to bottom, starting with a fabric B triangle. To make the third row, sew 9 background triangles and 8 fabric C triangles together top to bottom, starting with a background triangle.

**3** Sew the first 3 rows together, pinning and matching up the points in the rows as you go so all of the points meet up (**Figure 2**). Press the seams open. Set the completed rows aside.

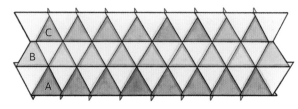

FIGURE 2

**4** To make the fourth row, sew 9 background triangles and 8 fabric D triangles together top to bottom, starting with a background triangle. To make the fifth row, sew 8 background triangles and 9 fabric A triangles together top to bottom, starting with a fabric A triangle. Following step 3, sew these two rows together and set aside.

**5** To make the sixth row, sew 9 background triangles and 8 fabric B triangles together top to bottom, starting with a background triangle.

## ASSEMBLING THE QUILT

**6** Referring to **Figure 3**, lay out the rows as shown, matching the triangle rows to each of the correspondingly sized background rectangles. Sew the rows together, pinning and pressing as you go. Trim the extra half triangles on the sides of the rows with a rotary cutter and ruler so the sides are even.

**Note:** *Be sure to leave a 1/4" (6 mm) seam allowance so you can sew the binding down later to make the triangles the correct size.*

**7** Layer the backing (wrong-side up), the batting, and the quilt top (right-side up), and baste them together. Quilt as desired. (The featured quilt was handquilted using 12wt thread with a running stitch following the diagonal lines of the triangles [see **Figure 4**].)

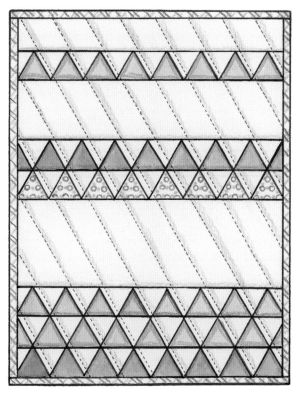

FIGURE 4

**8** Bind the quilt.

*For tips and detailed instructions on how to finish your quilt, turn to Chapter Ten: Putting It All Together.*

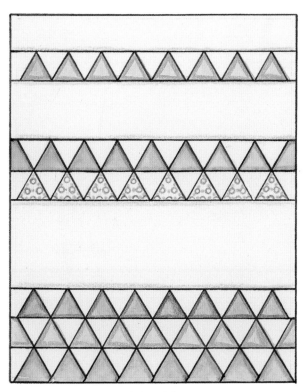

FIGURE 3

# Pond Ripples Pillow

Equilateral triangles make modern geometric patterns. They can be easily transformed to make different designs by changing the direction of the triangles or the grouping of colors. This design can be made with many options, such as a limited color selection or using fabric scraps for a completely different look. Solids would also look great. You could even use a jelly roll bundle for this design.

## MATERIALS

Assorted prints, 9 fat eighths
(each 9" × 21" [23 cm × 53.5 cm])

Background fabric, 1/2 yard (0.5 m)

Pillow backing fabric, 2/3 yard (0.6 m)

Binding fabric, 1/4 yard (0.2 m)

Batting, 30" (76 cm) square

Zipper, 22" (56 cm)

Pillow insert, 22" (56 cm) square

60-degree equilateral triangle ruler

**Finished Size:**
22½" (57 cm) square

**FAT-EIGHTH AND JELLY-ROLL FRIENDLY**

*All seam allowances are ¼" (6 mm)*
*unless otherwise noted.*

## CUTTING INSTRUCTIONS

**Note:** *If you're planning on rotary cutting with an equilateral triangle ruler that does not have clipped off tips, increase the width of the strips from 2½" (6.5 cm) to 2¾" (7 cm).*

**From each of the 9 prints, cut:**
(1) 2½" (6.5 cm) × WOF (width-of-fabric) strip; subcut into 12 triangles per print (108 triangles total)

**From the background fabric, cut:**
(6) 2½" (6.5 cm) × WOF strips; subcut into (112) 2½" (6.5 cm) triangles

**From the backing fabric, cut:**
(1) 4¾" × 22½" (12 cm × 57 cm) strip

(1) 20¼" × 22½" (51.5 cm × 57 cm) strip

**From the binding fabric, cut:**
(3) 2½" (6.5 cm) × WOF strips

## MAKING THE ROWS

For detailed directions, see How to Make Equilateral Triangles at the beginning of Chapter Six.

**1** On a flat surface, arrange the print triangles and background triangles as shown (see **Figure 4**)— or until you are happy with the fabric color and print arrangement. There should be 20 whole triangles per row.

**2** Pin and sew the triangles in the first row together top to bottom (**Figure 1**).

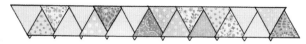

FIGURE 1

**3** Continue sewing the rows together in the same manner as step 2 until you have 11 sewn rows (Figure 2).

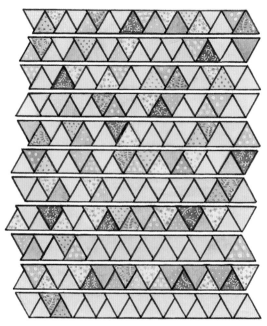

FIGURE 2

## ASSEMBLING THE PILLOW

**4** Pin the first and second rows together with right sides together, lining up the points as you go so all the points meet. Sew the rows together, pressing the seams open (**Figure 3**).

FIGURE 3

**5** Continue pinning and sewing the rows together in pairs until they are all sewn together (**Figure 4**). The sides can be trimmed before quilting to allow for a ¼" (6 mm) seam allowance.

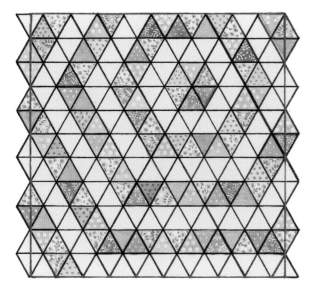

FIGURE 4

**6** Layer the batting and pillow top, and baste. Machine quilt as desired. (The featured pillow was machine-quilted following the diagonal lines of the triangles.)

**7** Add the backing and zipper. For instructions, see Making a Pillow Backing With a Zipper in Chapter Ten.

**8** Bind the pillow cover. Fill with the pillow insert.

*For tips and detailed instructions on how to finish your pillow, turn to Chapter Ten: Putting It All Together.*

# CHAPTER 7

# English Paper Piecing

English paper piecing (EPP) is the technique of basting fabric around precut paper shapes so the shapes can be more easily sewn together by hand. This traditional quilting method has experienced a modern resurgence mainly due to readily available precut shapes that come in a variety of designs, including hexagons, diamonds, apple cores, and equilateral triangles. But once you've mastered this technique, you can apply it to any shape you choose.

In this chapter, you'll learn how to baste and stitch shapes together with simple handsewing techniques. You will also discover the best tools and supplies to use. Good-quality cotton thread is important for EPP as there is little point in spending so much time handsewing only to have poor-quality thread snap, shred, or twist on you. This will leave you frustrated and potentially with holes in your sewing from the broken threads.

Handsewing needles are a personal choice. My favorite to use are Size 9 appliqué/sharp needles. They have a little bit of flexibility but are strong enough to work through fabric and paper. The length of the needle is just right and comfortable to hold. Some quilters like to use milliners needles, which are long and very flexible. You may need to experiment to figure out which needle you feel the most comfortable working with and can control well.

# How to English Paper Piece

If you use a glue pen to baste the fabric to the precut papers, make sure it is of archival quality so it does not bleach or ruin the fabric.

## MATERIALS

Fabric

Precut English paper piecing papers

Thread and needles (I prefer Aurifil 50wt cotton thread and Clover Black Gold Needles Applique/Sharps No. 9)

Glue pen (archival quality)

Binding clips (optional)

Rotary cutter

Self-healing mat

Acrylic template (the template should be about ½" [1.3 cm] larger than the corresponding precut paper)

**1** Set the acrylic template on top of the fabric. Using a rotary cutter, cut the fabric around the template (**Figure 1**). Repeat this process to cut out the required number of fabric shapes for your project.

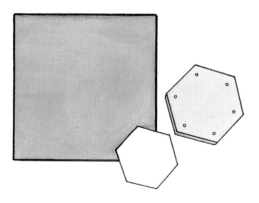

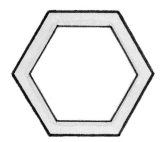

FIGURE 1

**2** Center the paper on the wrong side of the fabric. Run a line of glue along the edges (but not too close) of the paper, then fold the fabric over the glue (**Figure 2**).

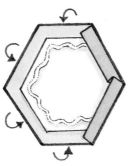

FIGURE 2

**3** Repeat step 2 for the remaining shapes (**Figure 3**).

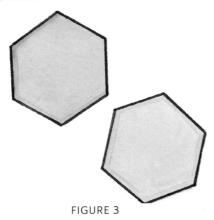

FIGURE 3

**4** Place 2 finished shapes right sides together. Using a whipstitch, sew the shapes together from corner to corner as shown (**Figure 4**).

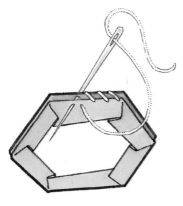

FIGURE 4

**5** Continue sewing the project pieces together with a whipstitch in the correct order for your project (**Figure 5**). After all of the pieces have been sewn together, carefully pull the fabric seam allowance away from the paper to release and remove the paper. Refold the seam allowance, if needed, and press your project so the seams are nice and flat.

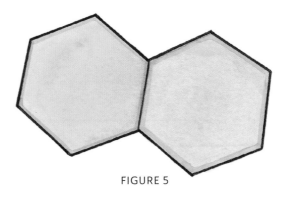

FIGURE 5

## author advice

### TIPS FOR BETTER ENGLISH PAPER PIECING

- Use a binding clip to hold the pieces together until you sew them.

- Try not to catch any of the paper when sewing pieces together.

- Knot the beginning and end of each seam. The tinier the knot, the better to prevent bulk, but it must be strong.

# Pentagon Bangles Table Runner

This colorful runner offers an easy introduction to English paper piecing. The result is a fun, modern centerpiece that will brighten up any table.

## MATERIALS

Colorful fabric for pentagon shapes, 10 fat sixteenths (each 9" × 10" [23 cm × 25.5 cm])

Background fabric, 5 fat quarters (each 18" × 22" [45.5 cm × 56 cm])

Backing fabric, 1½ yards (1.4 m)

Binding fabric, ⅓ yard (0.3 m)

Batting, 26" × 53" (66 cm × 134.5 cm)

Precut paper pentagons, (50) 1½" (3.8 cm) pieces

Cotton thread and handsewing needles

Glue pen (archival quality)

Binding clips (optional)

Rotary cutter

Self-healing mat

Appliqué pins

Acrylic pentagon template, 2" (5 cm)

**Finished Size:**
18½" × 45½" (47 cm × 115.5 cm)

**Finished Block Size:**
9" (23 cm) square

**FAT-QUARTER FRIENDLY**

*All seam allowances are ¼" (6 mm) unless otherwise noted.*

## CUTTING INSTRUCTIONS

**From each of the 10 colorful fabrics, cut:**
5 pentagons (using the acrylic template, rotary cutter, and mat) (50 total)

**From each of the 5 background fabrics, cut:**
(2) 9½" (24 cm) squares (10 total)

**From the binding fabric, cut:**
(4) 2½" (6.5 cm) × WOF (width-of-fabric) strips

## MAKING THE BLOCKS

For detailed directions, see How to English Paper Piece at the beginning of Chapter Seven.

**1** Attach 1 precut paper pentagon to each of the 50 fabric pentagons.

**2** Handsew the pentagons together in arcs of 5, leaving out the seam allowance on the bottom of the first and last pentagon (**Figure 1**).

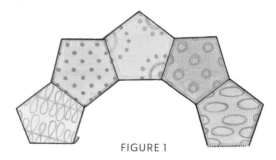

FIGURE 1

**3** Place a finished arc along one raw edge of a 9½" (24 cm) background square. Pin the arc in place so the raw edge of the first and last pentagons are lined up on the raw edge of the background fabric (**Figure 2**).

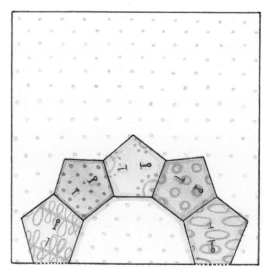

FIGURE 2

**4** Sew the arc in place using an appliqué stitch along the sides of the pentagons (**Figure 3**).

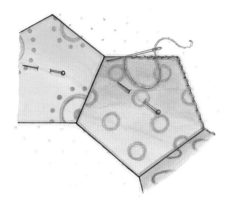

FIGURE 3

**5** Make 10 blocks.

## ASSEMBLING THE RUNNER

**6** Arrange the blocks in 2 rows as shown (**Figure 4**).

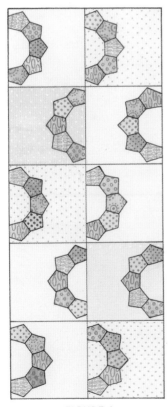

FIGURE 4

**7** Pin and sew together the first row of blocks, pressing seams to the left. Sew the blocks in the second row together, pressing the seams to the right. Sew the two rows together, pressing the seams open.

**8** Layer the backing (wrong-side up), the batting, and the quilt top (right-side up), and baste them together. Quilt as desired. (The featured runner was quilted by machine sewing through the seams of the blocks and around the shape of the pentagon bangles.)

**9** Bind the runner.

*For tips and detailed instructions on how to finish your runner, turn to Chapter Ten: Putting It All Together.*

*For tips and detailed instructions on how to finish your runner, turn to Chapter Ten: Putting It All Together.*

## author advice

### MAKE IT REVERSIBLE

The featured table runner was made reversible by using a matching background fabric for the backing and sewing together 2 pentagon arcs, made from leftover fabrics, to form a circle. The circle was handsewn in place on the back after the quilting of the table runner was complete.

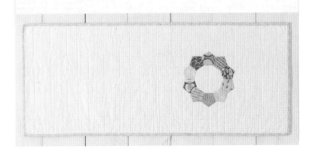

# All About Hex Pillow

Fussy cutting fabric is a great way to show off fabric designs. So many fabric collections use designers' creations as works of art, and these designs often lend themselves to being cut out to showcase the actual prints within a fabric. Fabrics for fussy cutting could include designs with birds, ships, children, or animals. Not only are these great for sewing projects for kids, but adults will also fall in love with these designs.

Using see-through acrylic templates will allow you to "artfully" fussy cut what you would like to include in the center of your hexagon.

## MATERIALS

Coordinating fabrics for fussy cutting*, (7) 10" (25.5 cm) squares

Coordinating fabrics*, (7) 10" (25.5 cm) squares

Background fabric, 3/4 yard (0.7 m)

Pillow backing fabric, 3/4 yard (0.7 m)

Batting, 30" (76 cm) square

Zipper, 22" (56 cm)

Pillow insert, 22" (56 cm) square

Precut paper hexagons, (13) 1½" (3.8 cm) pieces

Precut paper half hexagons, (42) 1½" (3.8 cm) pieces

Cotton thread and handsewing needles

Glue pen (archival quality)

Binding clips (optional)

Appliqué pins

Rotary cutter and mat

Acrylic hexagon template, 2" (5 cm)

Acrylic half-hexagon template, 2" (5 cm)

**Finished Size:**
22½" (57 cm) square

*\* The quantity of fabric squares required for this project will vary by fabric. The fussy-cut fabrics for this All About Hex Pillow were made from a layer cake of fabrics from the Tiger Lily line by Heather Ross. But a fat eighth of fabric is a good starting point.*

*All seam allowances are 1/4" (6 mm) unless otherwise noted.*

## CUTTING INSTRUCTIONS

**From 1 fussy-cut fabric square (for the center hexagon), cut:**
1 hexagon using the acrylic template

**From each of the remaining 6 fussy-cut fabric squares, cut:**
2 hexagons using the acrylic template

**From 1 coordinating square (for the center half hexagons), cut:**
6 half hexagons using the acrylic template

**From each of 6 coordinating squares, cut:**
6 half hexagons using the acrylic template

**From the background fabric, cut:**
(1) 22½″ (57 cm) square

**From the backing fabric, cut:**
(1) 4¾" × 22½" (12 cm × 57 cm) rectangle

(1) 20¼" × 22½" (51.5 cm × 57 cm) strip

## MAKING THE BLOCKS

For detailed directions, see How to English Paper Piece at the beginning of Chapter Seven.

**1** Attach the fabric shapes to the coordinating pre-cut paper hexagons and half hexagons (**Figure 1**).

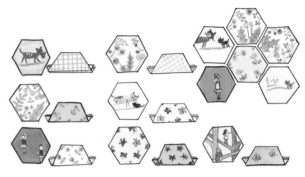

FIGURE 1

**2** Set aside 6 fussy-cut hexagons. Press the hexagons. These will be used in step 6.

**3** Handsew 6 coordinating half hexagons to 1 hexagon (**Figure 2**). Start with a single fussy-cut hexagon in the center and work your way around the sides. Make 7 of these larger hexagons.

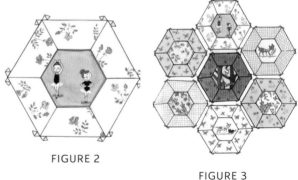

FIGURE 2

FIGURE 3

**4** Arrange the larger hexagons in a pattern as shown (**Figure 3**).

**5** Handsew the larger hexagons together in the same manner as before (**Figure 4**). Start with the single fussy cut-hexagon as your center and work your way around.

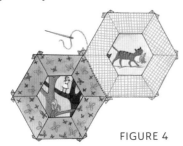

FIGURE 4

**6** Press the completed hexagon centerpiece, then carefully remove the papers. Re-press the seams back into place, if needed (**Figure 5**).

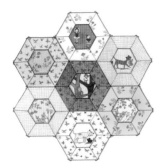

FIGURE 5

**7** Set the completed hexagon centerpiece in the middle of the background fabric, securing it in place with appliqué pins. Arrange the remaining hexagons around the centerpiece, leaving about 3/4" (2 cm) between the shapes.

**8** Sew the large hexagon centerpiece and small hexagons in place along the sides with an appliqué stitch (**Figure 6**), tucking under any stray tips from the half hexagons (**Figure 7**). Press the pillow top.

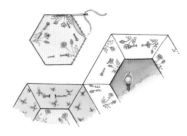

FIGURE 6

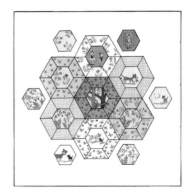

FIGURE 7

## ASSEMBLING THE PILLOW

**9** Layer the batting and pillow top, then baste around the edges. Quilt as desired. (The featured pillow was handquilted using matching colored threads around the hexagons and handquited diagonal lines across the background fabric [**Figure 8**]).

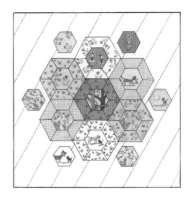

FIGURE 8

**10** Add the backing and zipper. For instructions, see Making a Pillow Backing with a Zipper in Chapter Ten.

**11** Fill with the pillow insert.

*For tips and detailed instructions on how to finish your pillow, turn to Chapter Ten: Putting It All Together.*

# CHAPTER 8

# Appliqué

Appliqué has long been one of my quilting favorites. I love each step of the process, from tracing and cutting to sewing. I prefer to use paper-backed fusible web when making appliqué shapes because it allows for easy tracing and cutting. Not all fusible web is the same, so you may need to experiment to find a brand that works for you.

There are many machine stitches you can use for sewing on appliqué shapes. You can use a blanket stitch to sew around the outside edge of your shape. Or you may like to create a raw-edge appliqué, which uses a triple stitch just within the shape outline (as shown in the Blooms Mini Quilt). I also love to handsew appliqué, and again you can use any stitch you like.

# How to Appliqué

You can try a variety of different threads to add detail to your appliqué. For example, use rayon thread for a shiny finish or a variegated thread for interest. Feel free to get creative.

## MATERIALS

Fabric

Paper-backed fusible web

Thread and handsewing needle

Applique mat
(heat-proof mat for pressing)

Mechanical pencil

Iron

Templates

## author advice

### USE TEMPLATE PLASTIC

Trace repetitive shapes onto template plastic. The reusable shapes will speed up the tracing process so you can avoid individually drawing each shape the required number of times.

1 Using a lead pencil with a sharp point, such as a mechanical pencil, trace the appliqué shape onto the paper side of a piece of paper-backed fusible web. Cut out the fusible web shape approximately ⅜" (1 cm) outside of the pencil line (**Figure 1**). **Note:** *When tracing shapes, make sure you trace them in reverse on the fusible web; shapes that are symmetrical can be traced without reversing.*

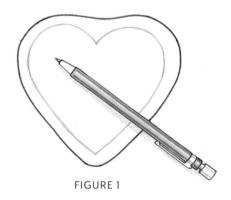

FIGURE 1

2 Press the fusible web onto the wrong side of the fabric according to the manufacturer's instructions (**Figure 2**).

FIGURE 2

**3** Carefully cut out the shape on the pencil line (**Figure 3**).

FIGURE 3

**4** Remove the paper from the back of the shape, then place the fusible web side of the shape onto the background fabric and press.

**5** Appliqué around the shape using your chosen stitch (**Figure 4**).

FIGURE 4

# Blooms Mini Quilt

The flowers in this stunning mini quilt will bloom all year round, and the sweet circular shape will fit any space. This is a great mini quilt to gift for a special occasion or just because. You can appliqué the flowers and leaves any way you choose to make this design match your style.

## MATERIALS

Print fabrics, 6 fat eighths
(each 9" × 21" [23 cm × 53.5 cm])

Green prints, 3 fat eighths
(each 9" × 21" [23 cm × 53.5 cm])

White background fabric, ½ yard (0.5 m)

Backing fabric, 26" (66 cm) square

Batting, 26" (66 cm) square

Paper-backed fusible web

Thread for appliqué and handsewing needle

Red bias binding tape (2½" [6.5 cm] wide), 1½ yards (1.4 m)

Fabric pencil or erasable fabric marker

Bloom appliqué templates (see Chapter Eleven)

Bloom appliqué pattern diagram
(see Chapter Eleven)

**Finished Size:**
18" (45.5 cm)

**FAT-EIGHTH FRIENDLY**

*All seam allowances are 1/4" (6 mm)
unless otherwise noted.*

## CUTTING INSTRUCTIONS

**From the background fabric, cut:**
(1) 20" (51 cm) square

**From the binding tape, cut:**
(1) 8" (20.5 cm) strip for the hanging loop
(optional)

## MAKING THE APPLIQUÉ DESIGN

For detailed directions, see How to Appliqué at the
beginning of Chapter Eight. Follow the manufacturer's
instructions for using the paper-backed fusible web.

**1** Trace the appliqué shapes onto the paper side
of the fusible web, then attach it to the fabric
and cut out the shapes (**Figure 1**).

FIGURE 1

**2** With an erasable fabric marker, draw a 16½" (42
cm) diameter circle on the background fabric.
Arrange the appliqué shapes in the circle (**Figure
2**). (Refer to the layout guide in the Pattern
Templates section.)

FIGURE 2

**3** Fuse the shapes in place, then sew around the
shapes using your chosen stitch (**Figure 3**).
**Note:** *The appliqué shapes shown here were
sewn with rayon thread using a triple stitch to
create a raw-edge appliqué.*

FIGURE 3

**4** Using an erasable fabric marker, draw an 18"
(45.5 cm) circle around the outside of your
Blooms appliqué (**Figure 4**).

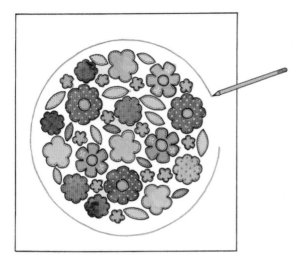

FIGURE 4

## ASSEMBLING THE QUILT

**5** Layer the backing (wrong-side up), the batting,
and the quilt top (right-side up), and baste them
together. Quilt as desired. Trim the excess fabric
away to leave the circle outline of your Blooms
Mini Quilt. (The featured quilt was machine-
quilted using a free-motion loopy stitch around
the appliqué shapes.)

**6** Referring to **Figure 5**, match the raw edges of
the bias binding to the marked circle line and pin
it in place. Sew the binding to the quilt.
**Note:** *If you want to add the optional hanging
loop, you will need to make and attach it before
sewing the binding down. To create the loop,
sew the long edges of an 8" (20.5 cm) strip of
bias tape in half, then fold the long edges in
half again. Pin the ends under the binding at
the top of the small quilt with the raw edges
facing out. Stitch the loop in place when you
sew the binding to the quilt (**Figure 6**).*

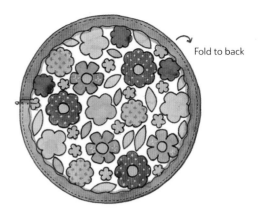

Fold to back

FIGURE 5

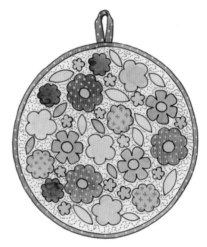

FIGURE 6

*For tips and detailed instructions on how to finish
your quilt, turn to Chapter Ten: Putting It All Together.*

# Love Pennant

Show your love with an eye-catching mini quilt. This simple red-and-white color scheme lets the words do the talking.

## MATERIALS

White fabric for the lettering, 1 fat eighth
(9" × 21" [23 cm × 53.5 cm])

Red-and-white prints, 5 fat eighths
(each 9" × 21" [23 cm × 53.5 cm])

Backing fabric, 20" × 24" (51 cm × 61 cm)

Red-and-white stripe binding fabric, ¼ yard
(0.2 m)

Batting, 20" × 24" (51 cm × 61 cm)

Paper-backed fusible web

Thread and needle for appliqué

Ruler

Pencil

Erasable fabric marking pen

Heart and letter templates (see the Pattern Templates section)

**Finished Size:**
12½" × 15½" (31.5 cm × 39.5 cm)

**FAT-EIGHTH FRIENDLY**

*All seam allowances are ¼" (6 mm) unless otherwise noted.*

## CUTTING INSTRUCTIONS

**From each of the red-and-white prints, cut:**
(3) 11⁄2" × 121⁄2" (3.8 cm × 31.5 cm) strips (15 total)

**From the binding fabric, cut:**
(2) 21⁄2" (6.5 cm) × WOF (width-of-fabric) strips

(3) 3" (7.5 cm) strips for the hanging loops (optional)

## MAKING THE APPLIQUÉ DESIGN

For detailed directions, see How to Appliqué at the beginning of Chapter Eight. Follow the manufacturer's instructions for using the paper-backed fusible web.

**1** Trace the letters onto the paper side of the fusible web, then attach it to the white fabric and cut out the letters (**Figure 1**). Set the letters aside.
**Note:** *Remember to trace letters in reverse onto the paper-backed fusible web.*

FIGURE 1

**2** Arrange the 15 red-and-white fabric strips as desired (**Figure 2**). Then pin and sew the strips together, pressing as you go.
**Note:** *Sew each strip in the direction opposite of the previous strip to avoid a "drifting" edge.*

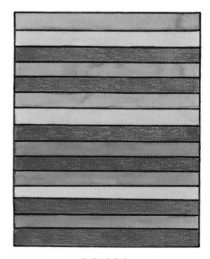

FIGURE 2

**3** Fuse the shapes in place (**Figure 3**), then appliqué around the heart and letters in your chosen stitches. (The featured pennant was machine-appliquéd with rayon thread using a blanket stitch.)

**4** Measure 10¼" (26 cm) down from the top edge on the left-hand side. Using the ruler and marking pen, draw a diagonal line to the center point at the bottom of the pennant. Do this on both sides.

FIGURE 3

## ASSEMBLING THE QUILT

**5** Layer the backing (wrong-side up), the batting, and the quilt top (right-side up), and baste them together. Machine quilt the pennant as desired. (The featured pennant was machine-quilted along each side of the seams, stopping and starting at the lettering.)

**6** Trim the pennant ¼" (6 mm) beyond the drawn line, along the sides and point of your quilt (**Figure 4**).

**Note:** *If you want to add the optional hanging loops, make and attach them before sewing down the binding. To create the loops, sew the long edges of the 3" (7.5 cm) bias tape strips in half, then fold the long edges in half again. Pin the ends under the binding at the top of the quilt with the raw edges facing out. Stitch the loops in place when you sew the binding to the quilt.*

FIGURE 4

**7** Bind the pennant.

*For tips and detailed instructions on how to finish your pennant, turn to Chapter Ten: Putting It All Together.*

# CHAPTER 9

# Foundation Paper Piecing

Foundation paper piecing is the technique of sewing fabric onto a foundation, such as paper, fabric, or interfacing. This foundation provides stability for quilting blocks when you're sewing across the bias (stretch) of fabric and will help ensure perfect points every time.

The technique may be a little tricky to learn, but once you get the hang of it, you will have another way to create a wide variety of blocks. You may also fall in love with being able to create blocks that can sometimes be more complicated than those designs sewn without this foundation behind them. Pictorial style blocks showcasing flowers, cakes, and people, for example, are especially popular with foundation paper piecing. But foundation paper piecing can even help you make blocks with simpler styles.

# How to Foundation Paper Piece

Set your sewing machine to a smaller stitch length when foundation paper piecing blocks. (I use 2.0 because it's easier to tear away the paper along the perforated stitch lines when I'm finished sewing.) Make sure to backstitch at the beginning and end of your sewing line to ensure your stitching won't come undone when you tear away the paper, and sew a few stitches before and after the start and end of lines that run into seam allowances. And always replace your needle after sewing on paper so you have a nice sharp needle for sewing the blocks together once the paper has been removed.

## MATERIALS

Fabric (requirements vary by project; great for scrap busting)

Pins

Rotary cutter

Ruler (I use the Add-A-Quarter but a regular ruler is fine)

Foundation paper piecing template (see Pattern Templates section)

Foundation paper piecing paper (regular copy paper also works)

**1** Ensure the copier is set for 100%—no size reduction. Copy enough foundation paper piecing block templates so you have 1 paper template for each block in your project. Trim the paper template along the dotted line (this is the outside seam allowance for the block). Cut the fabrics as directed, leaving at least a 3⁄8" (1 cm) margin around all sides.

**2** Place the paper template face up on the wrong side of fabric 1 (**Figure 1**). Pin the pieces together through the center. Align the fabric 2 piece right-side up along the side where the sew line is with the seam allowance about 1⁄4" (6 mm) outside the sew line. Pin in place (**Figure 2**). **Note:** *You will be sewing on the back of the block along the printed lines*

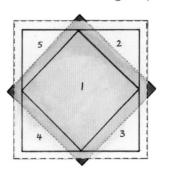

FIGURE 1

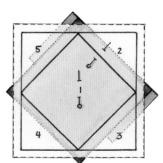

FIGURE 2

**3** Stitch along the sew line remembering to sew a few stitches before and after the stitch line and to backstitch at the beginning and end of each stitch line.

**4** Fold back the paper at the sewn line. Using a ruler and rotary cutter, trim any fabric overhanging the ruler to ¼" (6 mm) (**Figure 3**). Open fabric 2 and finger press it back over the seam line. From the front, the block will resemble **Figure 4**.

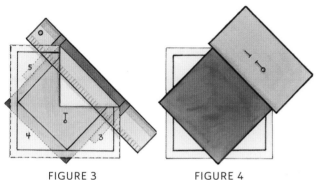

FIGURE 3          FIGURE 4

**5** Place the fabric 3 piece with the right side facing fabric 1 and lined up ¼" (6 mm) past the sewing line. Pin in place (**Figure 5**). Sew along the line.

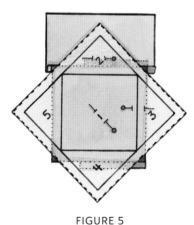

FIGURE 5

**6** Fold back the paper at the sewn line. Trim any fabric overhanging the ruler with the rotary cutter (**Figure 6**).

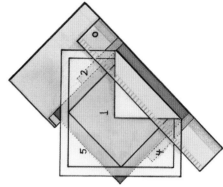

FIGURE 6

**7** Continue to move around your block, sewing the fabric pieces in number order, trimming and pinning as you go (**Figure 7**). From the back, the finished block will resemble **Figure 8**.

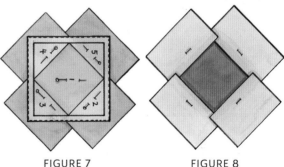

FIGURE 7          FIGURE 8

**8** Press the block carefully and trim the edges of the block to fit the dotted line of your template (**Figure 9**). Gently remove the paper from the back and sew the blocks together as directed.

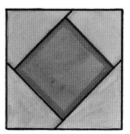

FIGURE 9

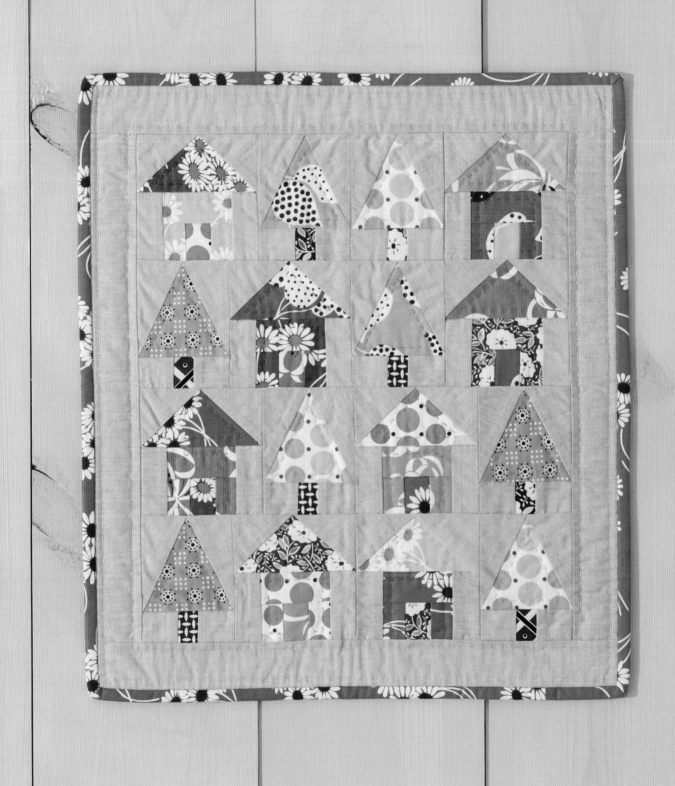

# Avenues Mini Quilt

Over the years, we've moved in and out of many houses. They carry sweet memories of experiences and events that have been a big part of our lives. No matter where I live, home is always where my family and friends are. This mini quilt celebrates those I hold dear.

## MATERIALS

Print fabrics (for the houses), 8 fat sixteenths (each 9" × 10" [23 cm × 25.5 cm])

Green prints (for the trees), 3 fat sixteenths (each 9" × 10" [23 cm × 25.5 cm])

Brown prints (for the tree trunks), (3) 5" (12.5 cm) squares

Background fabric, 5/8 yard (0.6 m)

Batting, 24" × 27" (61 cm × 68.5 cm)

Backing fabric, 3/4 yard (0.7 m)

Binding fabric, 1/4 yard (0.2 m)

Foundation masters; print 8 houses and 8 trees (see Pattern Templates section)

**Finished Size:**
17½" × 19½" (44.5 cm × 49.5 cm)

**Finished House Block Size:**
4" (10 cm) square

**Finished Tree Block Size:**
3" × 4" (7.5 cm × 10 cm)

**FAT-SIXTEENTH FRIENDLY**

*All seam allowances are ¼" (6 mm) unless otherwise noted.*

## CUTTING INSTRUCTIONS

### HOUSES:

From each of the 8 fat sixteenths, cut:

(1) 1½" × 2" (3.8 cm × 5 cm) strip (Piece 1)

(2) 1½" × 2" (3.8 cm × 5 cm) strips (Pieces 2, 3)

(1) 2" × 3½" (5 cm × 9 cm) strip (Piece 4)

(1) 2½" × 5" (6.5 cm × 12.5 cm) rectangle (Piece 7)

From the background fabric, cut:

(16) 2" × 3½" (5 cm × 9 cm) strips (Pieces 5, 6)

(16) 3" × 3½" (7.5 cm × 9 cm) strips (Pieces 8, 9)

### TREES:

From the green prints, cut:

(8) 3" × 4½" (7.5 cm × 11.5 cm) strips (Piece 4)

From the brown prints, cut:

(8) 1½" × 1¾" (3.8 cm × 4.5 cm) strips (Piece 1)

From the background fabric, cut:

(16) 2½" (6.5 cm) squares (Pieces 2, 3)

(16) 2½" × 4½" (6.5 cm × 11.5 cm) rectangles (Pieces 5, 6)

(2) 2" × 16½" (5 cm × 42 cm) strips for side borders

(2) 2" × 17½" (5 cm × 44.5 cm) strips for top/bottom borders

From the binding fabric, cut:

(2) 2½" (6.5 cm) × WOF (width-of-fabric) strips

## MAKING THE BLOCKS

For detailed directions, see How to Foundation Paper Piece at the beginning of Chapter Nine.

**1** Cut out the house and tree masters along the dotted lines.

**2** Make 8 house blocks using a combination of print and background fabrics (**Figure 1**). For each house, use 1 print for the door (piece 1), a second print for the walls (pieces 2, 3, and 4), and a third print for the roof (piece 7). Make 8 House blocks.

FIGURE 1

**3** Referring to **Figure 2**, make 8 Tree blocks with the 3 green prints (piece 4) and 3 brown prints (piece 1).

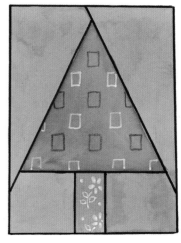

FIGURE 2

## ASSEMBLING THE QUILT

**4** Arrange the blocks as shown, alternating 2 House blocks and 2 Tree blocks in each row (**Figure 3**).

FIGURE 3

**5** Referring to **Figure 4**, sew the blocks together in each row, pinning and pressing the seams open. Then sew the rows together, pinning and pressing the seams open. The quilt center should measure 14½" × 16½" (37 cm × 42 cm).

FIGURE 4

**6** Referring to **Figure 5**, pin and sew a side border to each side of the quilt center, pressing the seams toward the borders. Pin and sew the top and bottom borders to the quilt center, pressing the seams toward the borders.

FIGURE 5

**7** Layer the backing (wrong-side up), the batting, and the quilt top (right-side up), and baste them together. Quilt as desired. (The featured quilt was handquilted with a running stitch about ¼" (6 mm) inside the seam allowances of the house and tree designs.)

**8** Bind the quilt.

*For tips and detailed instructions on how to finish your quilt, turn to Chapter Ten: Putting It All Together.*

# Sparkles Mini Quilt

Making this colorful project is great way to use up smaller pieces of your favorite fabrics as well as scraps. Although the foundation masters are the same, they are made up of different combinations of fabrics to create a striking effect for this project.

## MATERIALS

Print fabrics (fabric A), 16 fat sixteenths (each 9" × 10" [23 cm × 25.5])

Background prints (fabric B), 5 fat quarters (each 18" × 22" [45.5 cm × 56 cm])

Batting, 30" (76 cm)

Binding fabric, 1/4 yard (0.2 m)

Backing fabric, 30" (76 cm)

Foundation masters; print 4 of Block 1, 8 of Block 2, and 4 of Block 3 (see the Pattern Templates section)

**Finished Size:**
20½" (52 cm) square

**Finished Block Size:**
5" (12.5 cm) square

**SCRAP FRIENDLY**

*All seam allowances are 1/4" (6 mm) unless otherwise noted.*

## CUTTING INSTRUCTIONS

**From each of the print fabrics (A), cut:**
(3) 3" × 4½" (7.5 cm × 11.5 cm) (48 pieces total)

**From each of the background prints (B), cut:**
(16) 3" × 4½" (7.5 cm × 11.5 cm) rectangles (80 pieces total)

**From the binding fabric, cut:**
(3) 2½" (6.5 cm) × WOF (width-of-fabric) strips

## MAKING THE BLOCKS

*For this project, A represents the prints and B represents the background prints on the paper templates.*

**1** Cut out the block templates along the dotted lines, including the dotted diagonal lines through the center.

**2** Following the directions for How to Foundation Paper Piece at the beginning of Chapter Nine, create each block with the print fabrics (A) and background fabrics (B). For each block, start on the left-hand side and work your way across the block, sewing toward the right (**Figure 1**).
**Note:** *Because you cut through the central diagonal line, you will need to treat the fabric as if there is paper behind this central diagonal seam allowance and cut accordingly (**Figure 2**).*

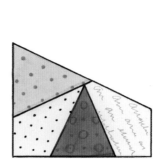 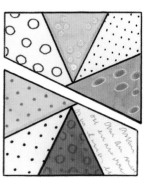

FIGURE 1              FIGURE 2

**3** Pin and sew the two halves of the block with right sides together, sewing along the dotted line so you have a 1/4" (6 mm) seam allowance through the center (**Figure 3**). Press the seam open.

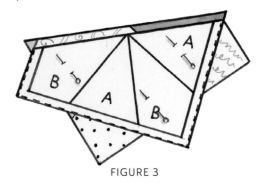

FIGURE 3

**4** Referring to **Figure 4**, foundation paper piece each of the blocks to make 4 of block 1, 8 of block 2, and 4 of block 3.

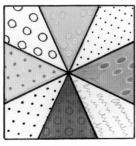

Block 1

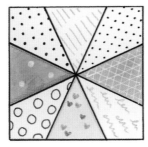

Block 2

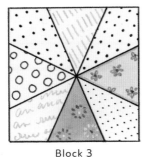

Block 3

FIGURE 4

## ASSEMBLING THE QUILT

**5** Arrange the blocks in 4 rows of 4 as shown. Pin and sew the blocks together by row, pressing the seams open (**Figure 5**).

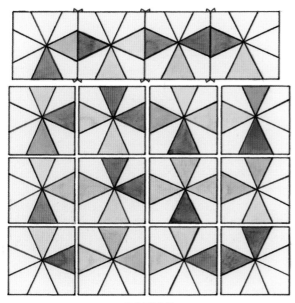

FIGURE 5

**6** Pin and sew the rows together, pressing the seams open.

**7** Layer the backing (wrong-side up), the batting, and the quilt top (right side-up), and baste them together. Quilt as desired. (The featured quilt was handquilted with a running stitch about ¼" [6 mm] inside the background fabric blocks in the star shape.)

**8** Bind the quilt (**Figure 6**).

FIGURE 6

*For tips and detailed instructions on how to finish your quilt, turn to Chapter Ten: Putting It All Together.*

# CHAPTER 10

# Putting It All Together

Once you've assembled the top of your quilt or project, it is time to put all the layers together and finish off the project.

With the instructions given in this book, you can change the finish of any project—adding or leaving off binding, for example, or turning a mini quilt into a pillow or vice versa.

Because I don't think of backing fabric as just utilitarian, I like to put personality into this part of the project as well. I prefer to use a fabric that will make the quilt reversible and a design on its own. I often choose fabrics with colors from the quilt front to make the back look just as appealing. Quite often the quilting design stands out more on the

backing fabric, so keep that in mind when choosing how you will quilt it.

I also love to use lightweight backing fabrics, such as lawns, for quilts. They add a soft feel to the quilt and often come in a great range of patterns. For pillows, I like to use heavier weight fabrics, such as chambray, linen, or denim, to give more structure and stability to the pillow.

When quilting your projects, you can add as much detail as you would like. If you decide to use neutral or solid backgrounds, for example, this offers a great opportunity to show off your machine- or handquilting skills!

## CUTTING OR PIECING BACKING

Backing fabric should always be about 4" (10 cm) larger than your quilt or project top on each side. You can either buy backing fabric that is large enough to be used in one piece or piece the backing together if you're using regular width fabric. I generally use backing fabric that matches the design of the quilt. Because the back of my quilts are often on display, I love to feature leftover blocks on the back or even piece a backing together out of leftover fabrics.

## SANDWICHING YOUR QUILT

To make a "quilt sandwich," lay the backing fabric on the floor right-side down. Smooth out any wrinkles, then hold the fabric in place with masking tape. Lay the batting on top and smooth out any wrinkles. Lay the pressed quilt top right-side up on the batting.

Baste the three layers together with safety pins. Starting from the center of the quilt sandwich, place the pins about 3" (7.5 cm) apart for handquilting or 4" (10 cm) apart for machine quilting. Work equally on all sides until you get to the edges (**Figure 1**).

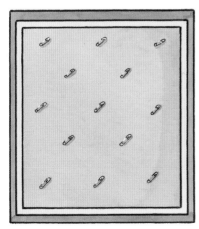

FIGURE 1

You can also "thread baste" the layers together using long, hand-basting stitches. Spray basting is another way to hold the layers together.

## QUILTING

I used a variety of quilting options for the projects in this book, including handquilting, machine quilting, and longarm quilting.

### Handquilting

This is a real love of mine. I adore the perfectly imperfect stitches you get with handquilting and the texture it creates in projects, which is quite different from machine quilting. I frequently handquilt projects that were handsewn.

### Machine Quilting

The machine-quilted projects use designs that were inspired by the quilt or project top. I like straight-line machine quilting, but also used free-motion quilting on some of the projects.

### Longarm Quilting

If you send your quilt out to be longarm quilted, as I did with the three large quilts in this book, you don't need to baste the layers together. Choose designs that reflect your project, and do keep in mind that longarm quilting can change the texture of your quilt. Heavier and denser quilting patterns, for example, will stiffen your quilt, while loose patterns allow for a softer drape. I like to choose patterns based on the type of fabric I used or that echo the design. You can use a floral pattern with floral fabrics, for example. Geometric patterns are great when these patterns are echoed in the quilt design. If you are unsure about what will best suit your quilt, ask your longarm quilter for suggestions.

## CREATING THE BINDING

Binding is the last step in making quilts and projects. It is the finishing touch that can add just the right detail. I prefer to use smaller scale prints for binding as long as they show in a narrow width. (I am a big fan of stripe bindings at the moment.) Avoid using prints such as large dots. If you miss the dot print when folding the binding, the dots may appear to drift off the edge or look uneven. Always choose colors or prints that complement your design.

1 To calculate how much binding you will need, measure the length of each side of the quilt. Add the numbers together, then add 10" (25.5 cm) to the total.

2 Join the binding strips by placing 2 strips at right angles. Mark a diagonal line from the top left corner to the bottom right and stitch along this line (**Figure 1**). Trim the corner (**Figure 2**). Press the seams open, then press the entire strip in half lengthwise with wrong sides together (**Figure 3**).

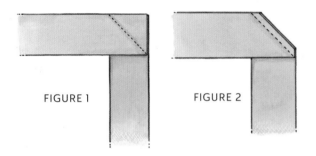

FIGURE 1          FIGURE 2

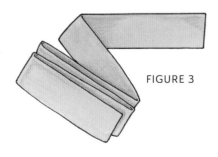

FIGURE 3

3 Starting about halfway along one side of the quilt, sew the binding strip to the right side of the quilt, mitering the corners as you go. To miter the corners, stop ¼"(6 mm) before you reach the corner of your quilt. Put the needle down into the quilt at this point and rotate the quilt 90 degrees. Reverse stitch back to the raw edge of the binding, then place the needle down into the quilt at this raw edge of the binding. Lift up the presser foot. Fold the binding at a 90-degree angle away from the quilt top and back, covering the angle you created. Line up the raw edges and sew along the next side of your quilt (**Figure 4**). Continue to sew around your quilt.

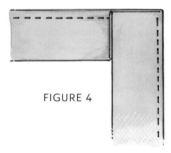

FIGURE 4

4 Stop about 6" (15 cm) from where you started. Open both ends of the binding and place the right sides together. Join each binding strip with a diagonal line as you did in step 2. Trim the seam allowance, then continue sewing the binding to the quilt top.

5 Trim the backing and batting, then fold over the binding and slip stitch into place, mitering the corners in the opposite direction from the front corners, along the back seam line (**Figure 5**).

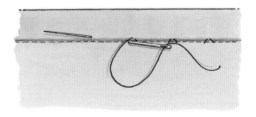

FIGURE 5

## MAKING A PILLOW BACKING WITH A ZIPPER

Using the materials from your project, follow these directions to create a pillow back with a zipper.

**1** Set the smaller piece of backing fabric wrong-side up. Referring to **Figure 1**, fold under 3/8" (1 cm) of the raw edge along one long side and press. Fold under another 1" (2.5 cm) and press. Set this top piece aside.

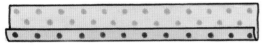

FIGURE 1

**2** Set the larger piece of backing fabric wrong-side up. Fold over 3/8" (1 cm) of the raw edge along one long side and press. Place the zipper face-up on your work surface. With the backing fabric right-side up, align the folded edge with the zipper edge as shown and pin the fold in place (**Figure 2**). Open the zipper a few inches.

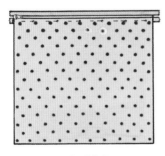

FIGURE 2

**3** Put the zipper foot on your sewing machine. Guide the edge of the foot to sew along the edge of the zipper. When you reach the zipper, place the needle down into the fabric, then lift up the presser foot and move the zipper pull past the machine foot. Put the presser foot back down and continue sewing to the end (**Figure 3**).

FIGURE 3

**4** Set both pieces of backing fabric on your work surface wrong-side up. Align the folded edge of the smaller backing fabric (top piece) with the unsewn zipper edge and pin (**Figure 4**).

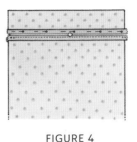

FIGURE 4

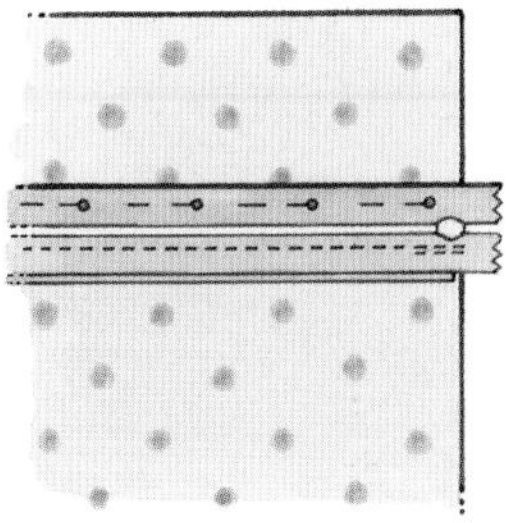

FIGURE 5

**5** Sew along the edge of the zipper, again moving the zipper pull and sewing as close to the zipper edge as possible (**Figure 5**).

**6** With right sides together, sew the completed pillow back to the pillow front as shown (**Figure 6**).

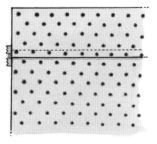

FIGURE 6

# Pattern Templates

## Blooms Appliqué Layout Guide

Layout guide is shown at 25%.
Enlarge to 400% to use.

When properly enlarged, this square should measure 1" (2.5 cm).

# Blooms Appliqué Templates

Make 3

Make 3

Make 3

Make 4

Make 3

Make 12

Make 3

Make 3

Make 5

Make 6

Make 6

Blooms Appliqué templates are shown at 50%.
Enlarge to 200% to use.

When properly enlarged, this square should measure 1" (2.5 cm).

# Avenues Mini Quilt

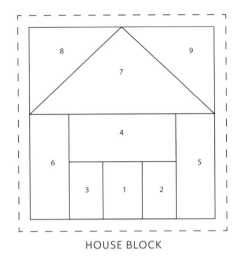

HOUSE BLOCK

PATTERN LAYOUT GUIDE

TREE BLOCK

House and Tree block templates are shown at 50%.
Enlarge to 200% to use.

When properly enlarged, this square should measure 1" (2.5 cm).

# Love Pennant

Love Pennant template is shown at 50%.
Enlarge to 200% to use.

When properly enlarged, this square should measure 1" (2.5 cm).

# Sparkles Mini Quilt

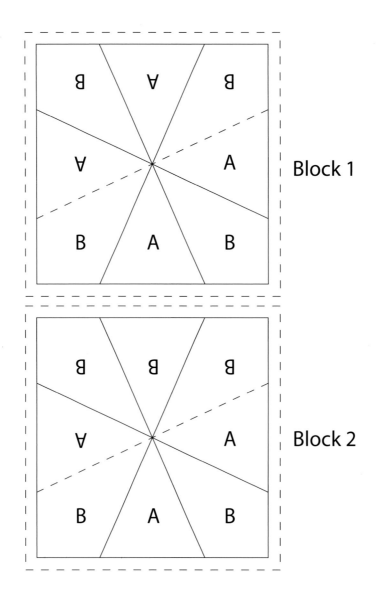

Block 1

Block 2

Block templates are shown at 50%.
Enlarge to 200% to use.

When properly enlarged, this square should measure 1" (2.5 cm).

# Sparkles Mini Quilt

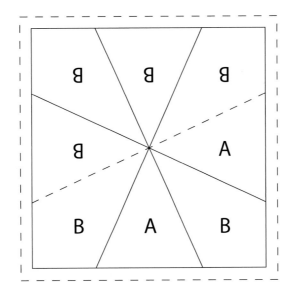

Block 3

Block templates are shown at 50%.
Enlarge to 200% to use.

When properly enlarged, this square should measure 1" (2.5 cm).

## RESOURCES

Carol's of Midland

www.carolsofmidland.com.au

Fat Quarter Shop

www.fatquartershop.com

The Strawberry Thief

www.thestrawberrythief.com.au

The Quilting Cottage

carolbradyquilting.blogspot.com.au

Aurifil Thread

www.aurifil.com

## INDEX

## About the Author

Jemima Flendt is a quilt maker and sewing pattern designer with a love for modern and contemporary design. With a professional background as a high school home economics teacher, she now teaches quilting and sewing classes and workshops and contributes regularly to publications worldwide. She lives in Perth, Western Australia, with her husband and two teenage daughters. Visit Jemima at www.tiedwitharibbon.com.

## ACKNOWLEDGMENTS

Firstly to my family, Ronny, Shay, and Ash. You have all encouraged me to believe that designing and writing a book was possible. A big thank you to Carol's of Midland, Fat Quarter Shop, and the Strawberry Thief for supplying fabric for the projects, and to Aurifil for supplying thread to make each and every quilt and project.

Carol Brady from the Quilting Cottage, you have done a fabulous job at finishing off the large quilts with your longarm and custom quilting services. To my editors: Amelia Johanson, you took a chance on this girl, and I am grateful for the support and hard work you gave to make this book a reality. Jodi Butler, you have been there to back up my ideas and make each of these projects truly reflect my style and love of quilting.

## DEDICATION

*For my nanna for nurturing, my mum for encouraging, and my girls, Shayla and Ashlyn, who continue to inspire my love of quilting and sewing.*

| Metric Conversion Chart | | |
|---|---|---|
| **TO CONVERT** | **TO** | **MULTIPLY BY** |
| Inches | Centimeters | 2.54 |
| Centimeters | Inches | 0.4 |
| Feet | Centimeters | 30.5 |
| Centimeters | Feet | 0.03 |
| Yards | Meters | 0.9 |
| Meters | Yards | 1.1 |

# Create beautiful home decor—and more—with these inspiring, beginner-friendly guides.

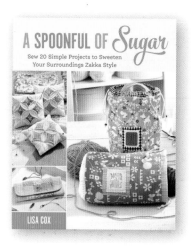

**See Kate Sew**

24 Learn-to-Sew Projects
You Can Make in an Hour

**By Kate Blocher**

$24.99 | ISBN 978-1-4402-4560-2

**A Spoonful of Sugar**

Sew 20 Simple Projects to
Sweeten Your Surroundings
Zakka Style

**By Lisa Cox**

$24.99 | ISBN 978-1-4402-4365-3

**The Simple Simon Guide To Patchwork Quilting**

Two Girls, Seven Blocks,
21 Blissful Patchwork Projects

**By Elizabeth Evans and Liz Evans**

$24.99 | ISBN 978-1-4402-4544-2

## Available at your favorite retailer or shopfonsandporter.com.

## Quilting Daily

For nearly a decade, Quilting Daily has been the place to learn, be inspired, and enjoy other quilters just like you. We bring you expert advice from our magazine editors, book editors, and Cate Prato, the editor of Quilting Daily.

**ERRATA CAN BE FOUND AT WWW.QUILTINGDAILY.COM/ERRATA**